ECHOES
OF THE
RAGING SEA

I0142181

No my friend, I may not know the pain, the loss
or the heartaches you have faced in your own raging
sea but I know the One who does. I pray you would
brave the sea's hell with the real and living hope found
in Him.

-Heath Christopher Goodman

John Norman
1980-2018
Loving Father, Son, Brother, Friend and Child of Papa God

Do you ever think of someone whose life was so animated and bodacious that to even mildly remember that they're no longer among us is like an anguishing spike being driven in the center of your soul, disrupting the ebb and flow of your inward peace, even if so briefly? It's so unsettling because you know deep down they weren't suppose to go so soon.

So many beautiful ragamuffins die before their time and leave a sad and haunting void in the living universe. Their lives, perhaps a real mess and yes, even sometimes to be sympathized yet they still managed to spread contagious life, color and flavor whereever they accidently crashed upon the scene.

This book is dedicated to one such ragamuffin, John Norman, keeper of the beard, a man of faith and struggles and leader of misfit toys in a broken world.

John was too young to die that's for sure. He braved to vanquish the raging sea but unfortunately the raging sea took him in a discouraging moment. But no judgment here, really... because if I understand God's amazing grace, He can turn any tragedy into hope. God alone can take a seemingly insignificant ragamuffin's single last teardrop falling upon the still waters of men's hearts and cause a ripple to be felt for all eternity...

ECHOES
OF THE
RAGING SEA

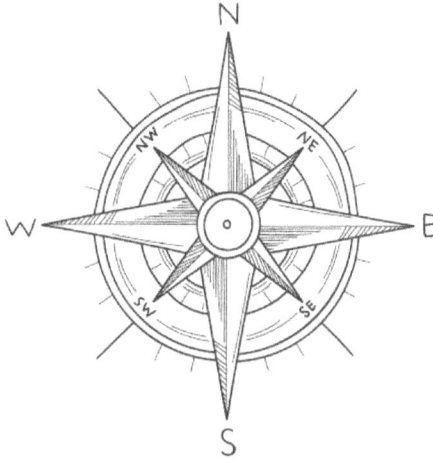

How An Incredibly Screwed Up, Depressed, Drug And Alcohol Crazed Teenager Was Miraculously Rescued From The Sea's Hell

HEATH CHRISTOPHER GOODMAN

CREATIVE
WORKS
PRESS

Leave Your Mark On The World.

ISBN: 978-1-951965-01-3 (Paperback)
Kindle Edition Available Through Amazon

Library of Congress Control Number: 2020900197

Any references to historical events, real people, or real places are used fictitiously. Names, characters, and places are products of the author's imagination.

Book design by CreatorGraphics.com

First printing edition 2020.

Creative Works Press
2001 Duncan Dr. NW Ste. #44
Kennesaw, GA 30156
404-307-9185
sales@creatorgraphics.com

www.CreativeWorks.cloud
www.CreatorGraphics.com

Book/Ministry Websites:
www.EchoesOfTheRagingSea.com
www.SavePreciousBabies.com

Preface

The raging sea, the teardrops of all humanity colliding together in a clash of sadness and suffering. Born into paradise lost, we all carry within us a residual memory from the first Adam, a memory of life, love and laughter where there were no tears of sorrow. An emptiness haunts every soul with this flash of imagery of a perfect world where death and suffering had not even been conceived.

No matter who we are or who we become, the raging sea within us and around us seems to crush any hope of a paradise restored. Death and suffering overshadow our brief time on the earth, as if we never really were here, as if we never existed. So what if we make a clamorous splash in the raging sea in an attempt to be noticed, to stand out in either infamy or fame? Are we not but a vapor, a single teardrop among an ocean of stormy waves, crashing upon each other in dismal vanity? What is our significance? What purpose or destiny does a teardrop have among an ocean of weeping?

But I have heard a rumor and found it to be true- there is One who transcends the raging sea and collects all our teardrops in a bottle...

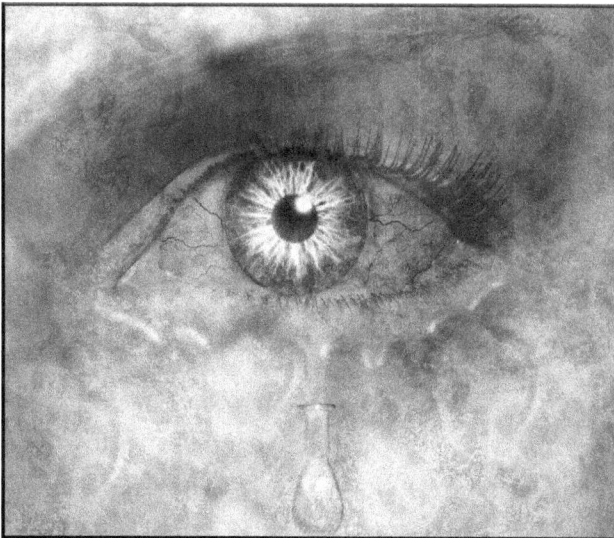

"You keep track of all my sorrows. You have collected all my tears in your bottle. You have recorded each one in your book." Psalms 56:8

Introduction

(You can skip this part if you really want to... but you might find intriguing some of my back story, motivation and somewhat whacked out reasons for this book.)

THIS IS ONE OF THOSE TEACHING MOMENTS

"Does everything always have to be a teaching moment, Dad?" My awesomely precious teenage daughter spoke these snippety words as I observed her from the rearview mirror, rolling her wonderful, bright eyes at me. I was navigating the car through the suburbs of Atlanta, through never ending traffic and praying for a miracle that the red sea of tail lights would part.

At first I thought, "Maybe she's right. I should scrap the rant I initiated and had all planned out for her glorious enlightenment. Maybe I should just chill out and be the 'cool Dad' that I always imagined myself to be one day to my teenager. We could travel down the road in sweet silence- me, engaging in a plethora of random (and sometimes off the grid) thoughts. Her, engaged in listening to Spotify while texting friends with cool little tidbits of teenage meme humor and Snapchat bravado. But no, instead, the Dad that sees everything as a teaching moment kicked into obsessively high gear.

"As a matter of fact, yes, every moment is a teaching moment and every moment is a learning moment too, Jordi. All of life is a teaching moment. I can pretty much look back at all my life and see that God was trying to teach me something at every freaking moment of my life! I didn't always learn what He was trying to teach me but I was being taught a lesson. Many times I had to retake the course over and over before I finally learned what He was trying to get through this little brain of mine, that fits so snugly in my skull bone!"

"Yeah, but I've heard it all before. You've told me these things a million times!" Jordi snapped back in typical teenage contemptible fashion and content.

I responded with sheer brilliance.

"Exactly! Sometimes God keeps repeating life lessons as we keep going around the same mountain expecting the promise land just over the same horizon! If we find ourselves on a not so fun merry-go-round, it's because we keep riding a plastic horse on an amusement park carousel thinking we are making progress. Truth is, we're only losing quarters in the giddy-up horsey machine."

I looked through my rearview mirror to see if my daughter was comprehending. She seemed comatose in the eyes but I continued on in parental madness.

"And you know what the definition of insanity is, don't you? It's repeating the exact same thing but expecting a different result every time. But if we learn the lesson or change up our ways, we move on to new things, better things, perhaps even the promise land." I spoke with great eloquence, authority and divine inspiration. I just knew she would see this and respond with hallelujah enlightenment and gratitude.

"I still don't think you have to spin everything as a school lesson or teaching moment. I'm 15 years old, Dad, I'm not a little kid anymore."

"See Jordi!" I had a super bright light bulb go off in my thoughtmobile. "Even you telling me that not 'everything has to be a teaching moment' is a teaching moment itself! Right now, you are trying to teach me, girl! You see, all communication and human interaction is based on the fundamental of it being a teaching moment!" Now I had my daughter in the awesome grip of sound reasoning. Surely she could not resist my great words of incredible wisdom. She would hang her head in defeat and surely acknowledge me as the greatest Dad and teacher ever to walk the face of the Earth!

"Whatever Dad. Watch the road, okay!"

I swerved back into the right lane, avoiding collisions and maybe death. I then gave up trying to convince her of my awesome logic and Dadness. "One day, probably when I'm dead and gone, she'll come around until then I've just got to keep planting the seeds of pure enlightenment." I pouted to myself. I then went off the grid with random thoughts while my daughter snapped her headphones back to her ears. Bittersweet silence ensued in the little white Prius... probably a teaching moment in itself somehow, if I had thought hard enough about it.

Okay, so some of you may just straight up be wondering, "Why is Heath taking the time and effort to write his life story out here? I mean, is his life really that interesting or the least bit intriguing?"

Don't worry, I asked myself those questions and even these- Is it to fulfill a narcissistic dream to produce a literary selfie, to murder innocent trees for a tedious biography that no one wants to read because their favorite sitcom is on tonight?

Well, to be honest, I do have a good reason why I keep typing away here, which I will share later. But first, I feel a "Dad rant" coming on. Forgive me, okay? I promise it will all make sense in the end... at least I hope.

I think one of the greatest strengths a person can have in his or her life is to know their weaknesses, to acknowledge their vulnerabilities and live in a constant effort to avoid them.

No, I didn't get that from a poster or meme. I actually thought it up by myself (imagine that), but I'm sure it's not an original thought. We have all probably formulated ideas that could be turned into an inspirational quote. Anyways, sometimes life happens and we can't avoid our weaknesses. This doesn't mean that we have to submit to the intimidation, then fall from our steadfast resolutions and wallow in the mud puddles of self pity. If we falter, if we fail, if we fall, can we not use even these as stepping stones to become stronger the next time, to be braver the next time, to be more prepared the next time? Can we not turn our failures into faithful guidestones, our fallings into launching pads to reach the next level? There's a scripture that says, "*For though a righteous or a good man falls seven times, he will rise or get back up, but the wicked will stumble into ruin and it will be the end of them.*" *Proverbs 24:16*

Why do some people become discouraged and fall off into oblivion? They shuffle and limp down the road of life, head down, spine curved, discontented, bitter, hopeless,wandering, crashing, burning?

And why do other people become discouraged in like manner? Then suddenly, they use that very discouragement to vanquish their doubts, fears and condemnations to propel them to final success and fulfillment- head up, spine strong, with contentment, joy, a hope and a destiny charted?

The difference is not the circumstances, or the draw of the luck, or some outward variable that defines a moment that can be blamed. The culprit lies within. We all have the potential for success and failure, for strength or weakness, to give all we've got until we succeed, or to give out and give up in utter desperation and failure.

I know both of these experientially. I have failed, sometimes very horribly, and succeeded, sometimes very unusually. I know what discouragement can do, both in a malignant way and in a benign way.

This book is a transparent look into my life. I can testify to experiencing discouragement as I curled up into a fetal position, lying in the mud waiting for death to "please take me". But I've also had discouragement that randomly propelled me towards Batman like powers and eventual success.

Yes, I admit it. Even today as a Christian for over 35 years, I still have my days where I want to crawl in a hole and just "pout it out" to God, the angels and my inner child. Yet, there are other days where I want to fly invincibly to the moon and back again as Super Duper Faith Dude. Some may call this a "bipolar" disorder (which I have never been diagnosed with). But I think it's a common human condition called "pinball living in a bumpy bouncy world". It's relatable with most of us who are not sterling gods of perfection.

I realize that depending on who you are and your current dispositions, you may find what I share in these pages somewhat foreign to your own perspective and disagree with some of my rants and ramblings. Some things may even seem offensive at times, given the politically correct, overly sensitive culture we seem to be living in today. After reading this book, you may despise me so much that you want to hire someone to assassinate me or chop off my only remaining fingers. (Okay, hopefully not so negatively intense.) I just ask you to please hold off with a final judgement until the last sentence has been read and you are staring senselessly at a blank back page. Why you would do that, I am not sure. Of course, it's my hope that you may agree and love what I share. Perhaps you will even become my obsessed, blind followers, almost worshipping everything I ever utter as the greatest truth and wisdom since Jesus or Gandhi. (Okay, hopefully not that overly positively intense either.)

Bottom line, I am aware that incredibly brilliant unbelievers among you may see this book as far too religious for your palate. You may smack down my references to God and the Bible as mere figments of my Newton. You might find a little or a lot of this book to be "so preachy" and that's partly because, well, I'm a preacher of sorts. But please plow through the scripture references and my attempt at wise sayings. Don't discount this crazy eyed, hillbilly, Bible thumper just yet. Humor me with your thoughtful and thorough investigation into my crazy world, would you? Even if it's just to understand where the freaky tarnation I am coming from. If you write a book, no matter if you're hailing Satan all throughout it, I'll read it to the end to try to understand where you're coming from, ok? Fair deal?

On the other hand, religious people may see this book as far too irreligious or "irreverent" for their sanctimonious, highfalutin piety. I know some have lived in such a prim and proper Christian bubble all their lives, that some of the stories/details of this book may literally shock the whitewashed smile off their churchy faces... or at least the fish symbol off their vehicles. Yes, I have not gone to proper "Christian etiquette" school, so if it seems raw and unrefined, well, it's because... it is.

Some may actually find it revolting to their form of "godliness" or "holiness". Please, if you find yourself questioning whether I am a true Christian or not, just say a prayer for me right then and there. Keep reading until the end. Maybe I'll get saved and become that super spiritual, stereotypical Christian you think I ought to be.

The Bible says *"A fool answers or judges a matter before he hears it to the full end." Proverbs 18:13*

I can only hope and strive that you will survive, unscathed by worldly corruption and still be very much holy in the aftermath of reading this book.

I would consider myself holy too... however, I think I would spell it holey because I'm sure there are still a lot of holes in my life, in my ever developing character and theology... which always seems to need mending as I look in hindsight. But would thou, oh man or woman of God, give me ear until the final text has zipped through thy filtering religious indoctrination? Then you may exercise thy most excellent discernments upon this lowly work, my spirit's discourse. Amen and Oh man!

All I know is, I am what I am by the grace of God... and by the "whack-a-mole" messed up life of trial and error I have lived... with and without God.

Some of the events in my childhood and life were downright tragic and disturbing. Try not to gasp with horror. Others were downright funny and random... I could easily turn them into a stand up comedy act. Try not to choke with disruptive hilarity. I am quite aware that most true stories don't fall into this morbid tragic/comedy genre. But I didn't write the script to my life, I just played the main character, ad lib, without a rehearsal. So if you feel horrified or saddened in one breath, then the next breath you feel like bursting out in ridiculous laughter, go right ahead. I won't hold it against you. No guilt trip for not expressing a moment of silence in between tears of sympathy and tears of laughter. I get it, really.

There are several reasons I chose to use the "raging sea" as my metaphoric life theme. I hope that I don't butcher it up too badly. Ever since I read the story of William Booth (the founder of the Salvation Army) and his vision of souls struggling in a raging sea, I have always been deeply moved by this analogy.

You see, I fancied my own soul struggling in that raging sea. It was more real than hyperbole. I almost drowned to "rise no more", but by the mercy of God, I found the Solid Rock, the refuge from the raging sea. This book is my personal testimony of how I was just barely alive, struggling, drowning. Then suddenly, "poof!"- I was rescued by an awesome, loving, tangibly real God.

I have shared bits and pieces of my testimony throughout the years with different folks but this is more extensive. Maybe after you've put the bits and pieces together, you'll say to yourself, "Okay, now it makes more sense why Heath Goodman is so undeniably odd and whacked out at times. I have always been worried about his mental frame but now I understand a little why he is the way he is!" The freaky weirdness totally explained.

Believe it or not, I'm still finding bits and pieces of my life and wondering why I am the way I am. I go to God for answers on my weirdness and my slow moving character development. He just shrugs His shoulders and says, "Be patient Heath, I'm still trying to figure you out too." Am I really God's Rubik's cube? Am I a riddle, wrapped in a mystery, inside an enigma, inside a human dilemma of a hypothetical burrito? Blink, blink.

Hopefully this book is not the definitive reflection of me... or the end of me. I hope, with God's help, to add a few grand and glorious chapters to it before I die... where I conquer worlds and slay dragons, valiantly living out being a legend in my own mind. At least that's the vision of grandeur that keeps me daydreaming at two in the morning. Or is that night dreaming? Or just too much coffee late at night?

Everything in this book is true as far as I can remember from my sketchy and volatile childhood and drug filled teenage years. All my stories and experiences are based on how I recollect them... which may be skewed a little by my faulty human memory, but by God's grace, I think I got it all right.

Also, I originally meant much of this book to be a last will and testament to give to my children and perhaps friends and family on my deathbed... to remember me by. So if it seems like I am writing my own obituary or last words before I die... it's because you never know what the future holds. Eventually, I will die. These words may be the only thing left that will testify that I was really here on this earth. (Now, please God, I'm not trying to tempt You to kill me immediately after this book is completed in order to validate my existential significance.)

I only compiled and converted my writings to be palatable to the masses when I decided to turn it into a book and publish it for the sake of more than a few family members. Originally, I wanted my children to get a better glimpse of who I am... or was. So that when they remember me, they don't think of me just as a worm city, six feet under and a bag of bones... but rather one hundred thousand miles high, up there with Jesus somewhere... doing something... maybe rag tag, or just maybe, mind boggling with Him!

Now every "Dad rant' or "teaching moment" that I might ramble on about in this book should be taken with a grain of salt. My perceived truth is perhaps "truth in flux". Meaning, I believe it's the truth at the time of writing it, but ask me again in a couple years. I might just change my position on a few spiritual and philosophical concepts... especially if something more compelling (based on how I read God's Word) comes to light. This may seem "double minded", unstable or whimsical to crusty theologians, who once they've been indoctrinated in their "truth constraints" they have never budged from it "for over 50 odd years".

However, I think truth is a dynamic process of growth, death and rebirth. Truth for me is not just a rainbow epiphany fixed in place that three angels have downloaded into my brain from God's Word. It's more like a plethora of layered ideas and perceived absolutes that construct or reconstruct pillars and foundations to build a whole way of thinking. But like the game of Jenga, where you can pull out just one wooden block for a whole tower to fall, I may be challenged to adjust my "truth" and find out that I have to scrap sacred cow fundamentals to allow for new revelations. Or what I would call "moments when God screws up your theology".

Simply put, I am adamant and unflinching about not being too adamant and unflinching... since I am finite, fallible and still forming.

Truth is line upon line, precept upon precept, here a little, there a little... and sometimes a bunch of painful experiences crammed in the mix.

I would hope that the truth I have come to know may not be so vicious and painful to you... but that in some way, transference could be achieved through literary osmosis, perhaps a little from this book as well as God's Word.

You see, academic knowledge usually just deceives us into thinking we know something when we have not even begun to scratch the surface of "real knowing". Real truth is solidified in us by way of experience and brokenness.

Chalkboard knowledge is always erased by the grit of indelible experience.

If I had to choose between a high ranking captain, fresh out of navy school with a high academic grade but no real experience on the high seas, or a petty officer with no academic training but who has lived fifty years navigating ships on the high seas, I would choose the latter with whom to brave a raging sea. This is because experience outweighs academia one thousand to one.

Now some might say, "Heath Man", what makes you qualified to write a book and to speak into anyone's life? What are your awesome, professional, man-made affirming credentials?"

Well, it's true, I don't have a PhD in psychology to impress others with my vast knowledge of Freud. (or is it Fraud?) Neither do I have a Master's in theology to use proper exegesis. (Or is that really "ex out Jesus"?) Nor do I know proper hermeneutics in my lofty Biblical explanations. I may not have those kinds of "credentials", but I know what God has done in my life, in my "experience". I may not know all the academics of the way the mind and heart work. But I am quite familiar with human nature, since I have a giant, fat one that I sumo wrestle with every single day!

I may not regurgitate indoctrinated theological concepts of such and such church denomination, but I do read my Bible plenty and in the raw (without a commentary to direct me a certain way). I do ask God for His enlightenment, not just relying on another man's interpretation. I too believe I have the Holy Spirit who God's Word instructs, *"Holy Spirit will teach you all things you need to know." John 14:26* Not that we can't be taught by men, but we should always set the priority for God to directly influence and show us the way. No middle man needed. No church priest, pastor or prophet needed for you to walk with God and grow in Godly wisdom. Oops, some church leaders might part ways with me here. They like being the liaison between God and men. I prefer you to know God directly as Jesus taught.

This may seem like I am a rebel towards institutional or religious education and maybe I am just a little. For all men, including myself are subject to error and deception. So it's always good to be suspect and cautious with corrupted and corruptible men. Eat what you may in regards to listening to preachers, teachers, educators, information and media indoctrination. However, in this confused and mixed up world, just be sure to ask Holy Spirit to help you discern truth from error and to "spit out all the bones"! *"Trust in the LORD with all your heart; and lean not to your own understanding." Proverbs 3:5*

Certainly trusting the Lord to discern truth is the greatest option. But what can also be a scary prospect is if you are somehow void of

Holy Spirit influence (mostly because of living in sin or rebellion), and you are merely being led by your own feelings and self-intuition that you ASSUME is Holy Spirit. Yes, you can get convoluted and whacked out by self perspectives and religious assumptions that you attribute to being God's own. Suffice it for now to say, Holy Spirit is a pure, holy, loving, patient, kind, selfless gentleman who never does anything that goes against the Word of God, or just for your own self centered agendas or justifications.

A sincere soul towards God will never be led astray like this. The true seeker will find Holy Spirit when they are humble, genuinely repentant, not self absorbed, who will diligently assimilate God's Word as their own absolute authority and truth... even when it hurts to conform to it.

So back from that rabbit trail- No, I don't have the shiney paper credentials that people trust in to "counsel" others. You ask, "What makes Heath qualified to help hurting, broken, raggedy, misfit people?" Four little words and a punctuation mark- Because I've been there!

I may not impress you with my vast academic forte, but I hope my heartfelt experiences and how God has worked in me would be of some value.

I still have not arrived on the plateau of perfection, but am no longer riding my high horse, snubbing my nose at less experienced ones. I am learning not to speak with ego and sanctimonious piety, or be condescending to those who may not have travelled as far down the road (as I may assume I have). Truth is, I am just a weary sojourner, traveling down the path, trying to put up some location markers and warning signs to help others not lose their way, where I had once wandered off the path. Maybe someone can learn from my mistakes, though I haven't even learned completely from them yet.

Yes, I am a Dad who likes to rant and rave with "teaching moment" material. I have randomly inserted them throughout my story here. Please, be patient and grant me my "Dad rants". If they don't spark a revolutionary enlightenment to own your soul, then so be it. Maybe I am not the great guru I think I could be someday with proper focus and flossing habits. I am a legend in my own mind, we'll just leave it at that.

16

Yet I am quite aware that I am human with a limited brain synapsis. I also know I am a flawed and banged up vessel who may not always get things exactly right. So please, sift through the dung heap of my story. Hopefully you'll find a diamond or two that God has buried somewhere in here. No, I don't claim to have all the answers or even know what the questions are... but I know someone who does. I actually seem to have more questions as I go along here. But I'm content to wait it out until "The Great Reveal".

TWO CENTS OF A RAGGEDY READ

To be honest, I really did not want to write this book at all. For over ten years, I thought perhaps about writing a little something on my life and testimony, but I struggled with trying to see the relevance of it in the scheme of my sphere of insignificant influence. It may seem like a ploy of false humility, but honest to God, I don't think of my life as a pertinent grain of sand that has any great contribution to make, or grandiose experiences that stand out in the vast shoreline of all humanity. Sure, I like to write but not too much about myself. Literary selfies are not my forte. I have written a few articles, a few social media posts about personal testimonies but nothing to this scale.

I have heard and read some really wonderful, powerful testimonies of God's redemptive work and incredible, miraculous experiences of other awesome, giant-sized Christians. Their books are worth reading... but in my estimation, my own testimony is perhaps quite ordinary and uneventful compared to the spectacular nature of others. Maybe there are some aspects of it that people can relate to or could be an encouragement... but why should I write extensively about it?

I have perhaps a dozen books I have never published, still in draft form. I have an over 500 page manuscript of Christian fiction I have shelved indefinitely. I authored and self published a book about my testimony of being an abortion survivor some years ago but it was not written to be palatable for the masses, I guess. What I consider normal logic, common sense and moral conviction sometimes appears to be radical and extremely passionate to those who want to stay cozy and cool in the current mainstream or "politically correct" environment.

I didn't want to even think about writing about my own life again. "God, am I that narcissistic to think that my crazy, ragamuffin life has anything to contribute to make a difference in this world?"

I love to write, but I just cringed at thinking that I could actually compose a book about my life testimony and that it would be worth two cents of a raggedy read.

Yes, I sometimes feel like I'm bursting at the seams to share what God has done in me. What stories I have to tell of his marvelous works-His teaching moments! To my wife and kids, they are "ragamuffin-Dad-on-a-tangent" stories. But what are they to others genuinely struggling in a raging sea? My sparks of enthusiasm might not be entertaining enough for a generation of screen fiend zombies mesmerized by CGI and Hollywood special effects. I don't have a particular song and dance to wow the crowd. So I just kept pushing the idea out of my head of writing my life's testimony. Until one day, that is...

One day I found out a dear friend of mine and Christian brother had lost his life in a tragic suicidal accident (I choose to "know" it was an accident). He was a handsome young man in his prime with a great future and destiny in front of him. His name was John. I had known him many years previously from the church we both attended. He was just a boy and I was in my early 20's then, but I took him under my wing and tried to be a friend and big brother to him. He had no big brother or father figure in his life at that time. We hung out, played video games and just had fun together.

I fell out of touch with John for many years after that. He grew up and became a young man and a father himself.

But I had recently reconnected with John on Facebook. We vowed to connect offline sometime. I knew John had taken some real hard knocks in his life. He struggled in the raging sea and was, like me, a ragamuffin in a raging sea. We chatted online and I encouraged him in the faith as he had re-dedicated his life to God. He had even written a beautiful testimony on his walk and faith with Jesus on a Facebook post. I knew he had bouts of depression and anxiety. He battled with being on psychotropic meds (which many of them seem to exacerbate emotional disorders). In my opinion, many of the trendy drug treatments will one day be frowned upon, like shock treatments and lobotomies, as primitive and counter-productive to the real causes of depression and mental illness. But who am I?

But John did seem like he was breaking through the fog and shadows of his life. I was so proud of him and really prayed and hoped John was on his way to transcending the raging sea in his life, that God was working miracles in him. I really thought we would meet someday soon, hang out and have sweet fellowship together.

So I was completely shocked when his sister wrote me... In a discouraged, intense moment, not in a right state of mind, John shot himself one night. He left behind a beautiful young son who will now only have fragments of memories of his father. I wept in my heart for my precious brother John and his little boy and the beautiful family he left behind.

I have learned in my life never to make a harsh or critical judgment of someone or something I know nothing or little about. I don't know all the circumstances behind John's accidental death, but I am sure of the mercy and love of an all encompassing God who loved John enough to die for him. John had faith in Christ but he was very tormented in his soul.

Suicide is tragic, and yes, many times it is an act of great selfishness on the part of the one who does it. Because they are not thinking of friends and loved ones left behind who are cruelly tormented, ranging from guilt, to fear, to total depression. Sometimes it leads to feelings of hopelessness and suicide in themselves. Suicide is an evil ripple in the fabric of a person's life, which destroys the happiness and tranquility of so many lives affected by it. I do not think it's a light or little thing.

However, we all do rash and selfish things at times. Sometimes the consequences are quite dramatically permanent, like suicide. But I don't believe suicide is an unforgivable sin by God. He sees the heart and circumstances behind the soul drowning in their raging sea. Remember, God's "mercy triumphs over judgment". His love and forgiveness is so extreme and unfathomable to us. If I am going to err, I will always err on the side of mercy. Sometimes people commit suicide in a dramatic way like John did. Others slowly give up on life, not caring for their bodies and perhaps eating or intoxicating their way to a fatal disease or drug overdose. Either way, it is tragic and so heartbreaking. I don't justify suicide or assume there aren't any reprimands from the Judge of all the universe. But I know the Judge personally. I love Him because He is so just, loving and merciful. I may not know too much, but I know that I know John is in good hands with the Father, who sent His Son to die for ragamuffin sinners.

As I reflected the night I heard of John's death, I kept thinking to myself, "What could I have done to save this young man from taking his own life? What could I have said or shared with my precious brother that could have helped him in the raging sea that so overwhelmed his life at times?"

I wish to God I would have been more encouraging. I wish to God I could have shared with John some of my own battles with the raging sea. When I was a boy... when my father abandoned me... when my father abused me... when I was lost and wandering... when I was bitter and self absorbed... when I was about to give up on life... when I felt the demons on my back... when the raging sea almost swallowed me up... Then somehow God pierced through the darkness and saved me in that moment! Oh how I wish I could have told John! He might still be here worshipping the Father with me today! I wept with so much regret but I know that I must do something now. Not for me, but in honor of John's struggle, and for all those "Johns" out there who need to know they are not alone and that others have braved the raging sea, fought battles like their own and have found a solid rock to trust in!

It was in my solitude with God, reflecting on John's passing that I felt God's Spirit say to me, "Heath, you have a testimony that others need to hear. You are a relevant, broken, ragamuffin in a broken, ragamuffin world. No, you can't save John. I have him safe and secure in My love now. But you can help to save others who might be able to relate to the raging sea that you have gone through."

I wish I could have been there more for John. But maybe, in some way, I can be there for him now by way of this book. "Lord, any good that may come of this book, I want John to receive the reward, okay? Really Lord, I'm not just trying to be super spiritual here!"

Can I pray that prayer or is that just creepy and weird? Is that part of my messed up Rubik's cube, wrapped in an enigma thingy?

I seek no reward for this book other than the reward of souls who might draw closer to the true and living God. I seek no recognition either... for who am I really, but another struggling soul in the raging sea who has found a beautiful rock and lighthouse to trust in? I was desperately lost. I found a compass, that's all.

So in dedication to my brother John, and the raging sea that swallows up so many ragamuffins like him in this world, I share with you my friends, my family, my brothers and sisters. Whether believers or unbelievers, I share in hopes that even if just one of you are touched and can brave the raging sea a little stronger, it will be worth it all for me. I share with all my love, mercy and grace extended to your soul, Here are just a few of my own thoughts and experiences... echoes of the raging sea.

A GODCIDENCE:

The Psalms 56:8 scripture theme of this book was prayerfully put in as a way to solidify the theme of my story. After sending the finished manuscript to John's precious mother to review, she wrote me back and told me that this very scripture was placed on his tombstone! I had not known this at all! What's the chance of that? I believe the Lord confirmed in such a wonderful way that this book will be used to help ragamuffins to brave their own raging sea! Perhaps you! Thank you Jesus!

ECHO: MONSTERS OF THE RAGING SEA?

On top of a very steep hill, surrounded almost entirely by forest except for one long, winding road going up to it, our isolated two-story brown house sat perched as "king of the mountain". It was an older house with fading brown wood siding. Only a newly built detached garage sat across from our flat, grassy front yard. Here, surrounded by an army of hickory, oak and pine trees, this creepy, lonesome homestead became the place where tragic and terrifying memories would be made. Here is where some happy, even comedic memories would also take place. Here is where the raging sea would shape my heart into a dichotomy of utter darkness, but also with a foggy, faint light of hope. There was no lighthouse nearby where we lived (metaphorically speaking), so it was in my childhood where I got lost without a compass, deep in the darkness, in the fog and crashing waves of the raging sea.

My father was not a monster. Really, he wasn't.

My daddy held the tip of the shotgun rifle up to the brim of my forehead. His eyes were bugged out and zombified.

"Daddy, please don't kill us! Please Daddy, we're very sorry! We won't ever do it again, please Daddy, we want to live!" I had tears running down my face as I looked over at my little brother Seany, who was also crying and shaking uncontrollably. As I knelt there on the floor of my father's bedroom, I was so afraid for us.

"I'm gonna kill both of you boys and then I'm going to blow

my own brains out!" My father angrily taunted as he shifted the point of the rifle between myself and Seany. He was sitting on his bed in a complete zoned out frame of mind.

My father's hair was all a mess, his eyes were dancing and dilated, as in typical fashion when he was running low on blood sugar. It is what I came to know and call an episode of "diabetic psychosis".

At 11 years old, I truly feared this might be the end of me and my little brother. We had finally made him snap royally. My father's hand was on the trigger as we, his two sons, kept pleading for mercy and forgiveness. "Please Daddy, don't pull the trigger... we are truly sorry... we don't want to die!"

My father sarcastically smiled and shouted out profanities at us. "You have brought me too much grief and disappointment boys. It's probably best for all of us!"

Our father's taunting and rambling seemed to go on forever.

But after an eternity in a moment, suddenly, "boom!" the horrific scene promptly ended as my father lowered the gun and shouted at us to go to our room. "You better hurry up and get out of here before I change my mind about letting you live!"

My brother and I wiped the terror and the tears from our eyes, sniffled and sighed with relief from the intensity of the situation. As quickly as we could, we made a mad dash to our bedroom. We had survived another one of our father's psychotic moments. We had dodged a bullet of being slaughtered by a deranged and destitute father.

What had caused my father, who grew up in a very proper Christian home, whose own father was a president of a prominent Christian college, who had been very familiar with stories of God's love and mercy, to now spiral out of control where he would seriously be tempted to take the life of his two sons and his own? What darkness and experiences in the raging sea had turned this lovable, sometimes graceful, goofy Daddy into the sea monster he had become? I didn't know but I thought he was a monster back then... but my father wasn't a monster. He really wasn't!

After Daddy had lowered the gun that day, I lowered much of the love that still remained for him. He was no longer my "Daddy". He was my torturer, my prison guard, my enemy.

No, I didn't die that day. My brother didn't die that day. But something did die within us that day. Something so very precious to all life.... something beautiful, innocent and wholesome was killed in that turbulent moment of the raging sea. Something that only a miracle could resurrect and bring back to life again. Could it ever happen? Who knew?

The whole reason we stood before the executioner that autumn day in 1978, and could have easily been one of those horrific domestic murder/suicide statistics was because of something so trivial, so silly really... and yet apparently so serious. Something as trivial as two boys who were tired of eating the same old stale bologna sandwiches at school.

You see, one day Seany and I stumbled upon our father's treasured and highly valued collection of silver dollar coins. We were promptly enticed to steal them one by one over a period of weeks to purchase hot lunches at school. We had always craved the warm meals with the nice desserts. Back then, school lunches were delicious... at least we thought so. The silver dollars had no value to us other than they were, at face value, only worth exactly one dollar. Ironically, just the amount to purchase a hot school lunch.

After several weeks of ditching paper bag lunches, we exhausted our father's whole coin collection and had to go back to eating bologna, the grub of peasants. Oh yes, we lived and ate like the sons of a mighty king for a lunch hour moment, but undoubtedly, the raging sea would call us into account for our petty thievery and base appetites.

One Saturday, my father went to admire his valued collection, perhaps to sell due to financial pressures piling up. But alas, they were not where he had buried them, deep within his bedroom dresser drawer.

So he immediately screamed "Heath and Sean, come here right now!" The raging sea began to crash upon us again... like it had many, many times before.

After several belt whippings and screaming episodes from my father, instead of just making an honest confession, my brother and I knew the truth would infuriate him to unpredictable consequences. So we made up a story about the silver coins. We told him that we took them out into the forest that surrounded our house and buried them in an abandoned log cabin. We proceeded with the deception and even took him on a wild goose chase all that Saturday morning through the woods, searching for a log cabin that was not there. No silver dollars were truly buried, having perished with the using.

Now to be fair, my father was severely diabetic and probably had undiagnosed circumstantial or temporary mental issues to boot. He could not go very long without eating or his blood sugar would tank. He would become a crazed zombie with some true psychotic tendencies. Although, I have never consulted any professionals on this diagnosis, as a young boy living with him day in and day out, I figured it out all on my own, no PhD required. "Go, run and get a box of raisins for Daddy or we might find ourselves bleeding, broken or chopped up into little bite-sized pieces!" My brother and I would scramble to the snack cupboard to prevent our demise.

Unfortunately, that particular long morning of climbing over rocks and trees, we tested the limits of Daddy's low blood sugar... and generally how severe diabetes and anger issues are a really bad combination. Daddy also slowly realized that a great loss had occurred to what he assumed was a secure financial investment with his silver coins. These things contributed to the raging sea momentarily disconnecting my father from reality and truth. In turn, the raging sea was released upon my brother and I by way of a sadistic shotgun put to our heads.

No, I don't know if the rifle was really loaded that afternoon, but I do know a bullet was shot into my little brother's heart and mine, and that our childhood would never be the same. We came to see our father as a sea monster in our raging sea. This is when a dark, dark hatred and seething bitterness began to really fester within me.

After the rifle incident, something completely snapped inside of me. Yes, I had been a mischievous little boy with a propensity for petty childhood rascality for a long time. But much of it was innocence from ignorance or just ragamuffin boyish stuff. But after Daddy put a rifle to my head, that sadistic terror on top of the years of abuse, drove a really morbid and sick, evil wedge within my adolescence.

But I wasn't a monster. Really, I wasn't.

"Seany, the only way we're going to be able to live with Mommy again..." I paused to phrase my morbid words "...we're gonna have to kill Daddy." At just eleven years old, my heart had poisoned to a sinister, toxic level. "There's just no other way I can see that we can go back to Indiana and be with Mommy, and Cully and Ally." Cully was our big brother and Ally was our older sister.

I looked intently and seriously at Seany, my younger brother by two years. He had a blank expression on his face. He neither seemed surprised or taken back in any way by my insidious statement.

"But how can we kill Daddy? I don't know how we could do it," Seany responded, shrugging his shoulders.

"I've already thought about it. I think what we can do is set the house on fire after everyone falls asleep. Since our room is downstairs, it will be easy for us to leave. We will pour gasoline all over the outside of the house and when we go out, we'll light a match to it and get far enough away from..."

"But what about John John, our brother? We can't leave him!" Seany interrupted me.

My heart had so darkened that I had forgotten all about our little brother, John John, who we both really loved. I modified my plans on the spot.

"Yes, that's right. I was thinking then that we sneak up to his room first, take him from his bed and then leave."

"What about Josie?" Sean inquired. Josie was our step mother and the mother of John, who we affectionately called "John John".

"If our plan is to work Seany, we will have to let her die with Daddy in the fire." I quickly responded.

Both Seany and I had hardened our hearts towards both of them, so much so that this plan seemed like a favorable one that we could pull off without too much regret.

"We gotta steal some gasoline from Daddy's car or the neighbor that lives below us on the hill. We can get enough to pour all around the house, then we can plan to leave that night. We must also tell the police that we were only able to escape with our little brother. But we can't tell them that we started the fire Seany! We have to say we don't know who did it, or maybe say we heard robbers in the house. Okay?"

I instructed.

Seany nodded his head slowly.

"If they find out we did it then we will go to jail forever!" I emphasized.

"Forever?" Seany asked squinting his eyes with some doubt.

"Yes forever! We might even get the electric chair! We will be considered murderers. We will never see Mommy ever again either. You can't ever tell anyone when we do it," I answered matter of factly.

Seany just trailed off in wandering thought.

Later that evening as I lay in my bed, I didn't know if my plan would work. As I kept thinking about it, I started to doubt that it was a surefire plan, no pun intended. I began thinking of other ways I could kill my Daddy. I could try killing him with a knife, but then everyone would know that it was I that killed him and I would go to jail or get the electric chair.

I had to have a foolproof plan where no one would ever suspect or find out about it.

I thought again about several ways which might be more clandestine. I thought about one that really seemed promising. "Tomorrow, I'll get Seany to help and we'll do experiments to see if it will work," I thought to myself as I closed my eyes, growing sleepy.

However, just before I fell asleep, I stared to the left of me at my wall where our bunk beds were positioned. I saw something like a black splotch, blurry on the wall. It had never been there before. What was it? As I stared at it, it began to shape shift with a slight animation to it. All of a sudden, the black splotch morphed into the explicit face of a man with a very pointed mustache and beard and devious eyes. It looked like the devil himself. The animated face began to laugh maniacally on my wall. "Ha Ha Ha Ha!" My heart was so scared and my adrenaline stirred. I put my hands to my face and rubbed my eyes profusely. After several attempts, it finally went away. "What did I just see?" I genuinely was freaked out. "Was that a ghost? It was so vivid and real. How could I have imagined that?" I laid there with my heart pounding so fast.

After a good while, I was overcome with drowsiness and finally fell asleep.

27

The next day when Seany and I were alone in the kitchen, I set out to reveal to him my new plan on how we could kill Daddy.

I took Daddy's jug of tea that he liked to drink out of the refrigerator. I poured some into a cup.

"Seany, we need to experiment with this cup of tea. We need to find some poison that we can put in it so that when he drinks it, it will kill him straightway."

Seany looked at it and nodded.

I opened the cabinet below the kitchen sink where lots of cleaning supplies and other chemicals were stored. I took out various products and smelled them for potency, to see how strong of an odor they had. I poured one product into the cup of tea. It still smelled very pungent. I was sure Daddy would smell it first before he ever took a drink. We tried several other products but to no avail. Every chemical gave off too much of an odor.

I sighed with frustration. "Maybe, I have to find something in the garage where Daddy keeps other poisonous supplies." I looked at Seany who was just there for the ride. He nodded and I poured out the smelly concoction of mixed chemicals and black tea.

The raging sea of my life with Daddy had taken its toll on my boyhood psyche. No longer was I just a lonely victimized soul thrashing about, trying to survive it's tumultuous waves; I had turned into a sea monster myself. At 11 years old, I should have been a rambunctious, innocent, American kid filled with wide-eyed adventurous imagination and dreams. I should have loved baseball, bike-riding and Batman. I should have had only fond memories of fun with my Daddy, step mother and two little brothers. I should have... but...

Instead, I was a sea monster urging my little brother to become one as well. I was a sea monster filled with bitterness and hatred for a Daddy I once long ago adored. I was a sea monster ready to commit murder and mayhem. How did I become this twisted creature in the great tempest of my childhood? What dark forces and ominous experiences shaped my adolescent heart into such a ravenous beast? Why did I think murdering my own father and step mother would magically solve my problem with the raging sea inside of and around me? Why did I sear my developing conscience?

Who knew the answer? The apparition on the wall? Was it the devil? And was he laughing with me or at me or maybe both? Yes, I was a monster... but I wasn't a monster, was I?

ECHO: THE WORTH OF PEOPLE, THE WORTH OF THINGS

Yes, what an awful reveal about my childhood, you say? You are right. It is an incredibly horrendous childhood memory that I wish I could completely erase now. You see, the raging sea can billow out the darkest waves upon the souls of men... and upon the souls of little boys... taunted and haunted by painful, sadistic actions.

The sad thing is, one small impulsive act of just pulling a trigger, done out of being temporarily disconnected by a mental/medical condition could have resulted in my father, Seany and I being victims of a horrific crime scene in the late 70's. One little opportunity to follow through and kill my father could have resulted in a devastating outcome for my brother and I.

I am perplexed as I read the current news almost on a daily basis now. Yet I know too well the reason why similar horrifying stories happen, where fathers or mothers snap and murder their whole family, or sons and daughters do fatal, unspeakable violence against their own parents or siblings. I barely escaped it myself but the truth of it is so incredibly sad. One of the greatest signs Jesus spoke concerning the last generation before His return would be that the majority of people would have hearts that "grew cold", without natural love or affection for others. People have grown even more and more disconnected from one another as society interfaces more with impersonal screens and virtual "realities". We use social media to buffer ourselves and become very distant from one another. Our love has grown cold and we have become a very narcissistic "selfie" society. We hurt others with no regard, and only stir up contention and drama to excite our desensitized, demoralized minds. Many of us are addicted to raw, violent entertainments from the slow degradation of Hollywood and the television. We have no moral compass, no empathy or love as we increasingly push God, common decency and human compassion out of our lives.

If all we are are evolved amoebas and monkeys, then "morality" or self governing law is just an option since there is no ultimate authority or accountability. If we feel like raping, pillaging or killing for the thrill of it, then who is anyone to try to conform us to a value system on human life, or suppress any of our primordial, beastly urges? In the 1970's the sexual revolution and the world were surely plunged into incredible dark and disturbing debauchery. Yet now, fifty years later, the darkness, wickedness and lawlessness are totally unconstrained. Many of us are still so naive. We don't have a clue on how deep the rabbit hole goes in this sick, twisted, perverted, incredibly demonic age we are now living in.

I only know this- If the God who transcends the raging sea had not intervened at the very next juncture in my life as a preteen, I am sure that I would have had a much more pathological, violent history and probably a tragic end. But God did have a plan for my life. The raging sea wouldn't entirely swallow me up as it does so many.

You see, someone was praying for all of us. This is key I think. My God fearing grandparents on my father's side, Woodrow and Marie Goodman, were praying people, interceding for their children and their children's children. I am sure of it. My grandfather was a very strong Christian, the youngest president of Wesleyan University in Marion Indiana. He was also involved with my Great Uncle, Watson Goodman's World Missionary Press Tract Society that

My Godly Grandparents

still to this day sends Bibles and scripture tracts all over the world. As their prayers went upward, God's providence went downward to pull my brother and I, and our father out of what was sure to be a direct and fatal clash within the raging sea.

From our pictures growing up, you would have thought my father and us "boys" were always a happy family. In the early years, my father was a strict disciplinarian but still a very lovable Dad. But as Seany and I grew from toddlers into adolescence, the crashing waves,

31

the shadow and fog of the raging sea began to break us down. My father first developed a bad habit of scolding and deriding my brother and I. We were "good for nothing". We were "losers", "rotten children", "stupid", "idiots" and "delinquents".

"Me & My Boys"

The angry words he spoke would echo in my mind like a festering splinter to my psyche. On top of the abuse I took at school from bullies who made fun of the birth defects of my deformed fingers, I was growing weary of being fearful and badgered by both bullies and my Daddy. I truly began to feel disconnected from being human or from being his son altogether. When I became a preteen, I began to feel like I was just a giant disappointment in the world, waiting to screw up one final time before I would probably die. Either that, or I would find a way to end my father's apparent miserable existence and go back to Mama's. One of us had to go. The raging sea between father and son had caused us both to gasp and thrash about, pushing the other down, drowning each other in our self centered attempts at "survival of the fittest" within the sea's hell.

The raging sea of this life is a tempest, many times because the creatures within it do not properly understand life's value system, and the proper order of worthiness when it comes to living entities versus non living things. All of life, the biosphere and ecosystem was originally designed to work in a beautiful, symbiotic relationship to one another, especially in regards to the value or worth of each of its members.

You see, my brother and I were foolish, ignorant boys for not recognizing the true worth of those silver coins. We saw them as a cheap, easy way to feed our faces. But children are full of such folly. They need encouraging and positive instruction to value things according to their true worth. As adults, we should know better. Sadly, many of us never mature in understanding what is valuable and what is not.

My father at that time, was not mature in his own understanding. You see, he was foolish and ignorant for not recognizing the true value or worth of his two sons. He placed a higher value on the things, the silver coins that he lost, more than on the sons that he still possessed. Surely we should have been punished out of love and perhaps would have learned a valuable lesson that didn't scar us for life.

But Daddy had a crisis, a meltdown and a moment when the raging sea within him would alter the childhood innocence of his two sons. As we know in this world, "things" or material objects can be replaced by a manufactured duplicate or a facsimile thereof... but people, no they can't! Silver coins can be easily replaced. Little boys, no, not at all!

Each of us is unique, precious, one of a kind. Each soul is always on the verge of going extinct, so he or she must be placed at the highest value or worth in life's ecosystem. We all must be on the "protected environmental status" list. For no two souls are alike and death means extinction of our own uniqueness. We should treat each person with this respect and value, no matter who they are or what they look like. No racism or hatred can manifest if we properly value all human life.

Each of us have a story of tragedy and triumph to tell. Each of us have our own experiences within the raging sea, either succumbing to the dreaded tempests before us... or surviving it, by treading it wearily... or transcending it in some glorious, God honoring way.

Because we are all victims of the raging sea to whatever degree, we should choose to be empathetic and loving to others, not hurtful and destructive, only caring about our own plight. The raging sea in me doesn't give me the right to drown others. Instead, it should be the very catalyst that breaks the cycle of the sea's hell. Since I have been a victim of the raging sea, I should be even more an advocate for the opposite, for good, not an extension of evil. Yet, human nature can be vindictive and bitter, to hurt because it's been hurt, to lash out in anger and violence because it's been the victim of anger and violence. Only human nature, the fallen nature, perpetuates the cycle of pain and evil. This only exasperates the turmoil and velocity of an already raging sea. What can turn the tide in humanity's plight? What can bring tranquility and peace to the raging sea of all our lives?

ECHO: A BRAND PLUCKED FROM THE FIRE

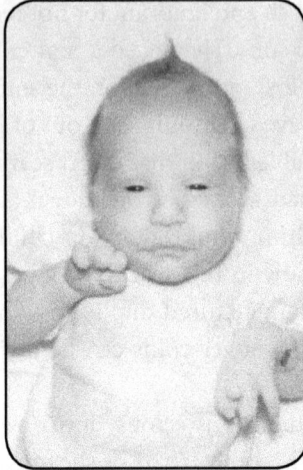

Showing Off My Designer Hands

Upon my birth, an indelible scar of the sea's hell would mark all of my days on earth as a bit more peculiar than others. A scar from a struggle that my mother had with the raging sea.

My mother was a cross between a highly intelligent bookworm/ socialite and a drug/alcohol crazed hippy who loved partying and skinny dipping with her boyfriend in the local quarry hole.

She had been married twice, before she married my father. She had one child from each of those marriages, Allyson Winn, the "Poo" and Cullen Bret or "Ceebers".

When she was pregnant with me, her marriage to my father was on the rocks. It looked like she was going to be a single mother again, but this time she would have three little ones to take care of.

This was a horrifying prospect for her and some of her friends had given her some "old wives tales" ways of having a "do it yourself" abortion. She was told that certain over the counter drugs could induce a miscarriage and she could abort me without too much complication. My mother struggled with this idea. She was brought up Catholic but didn't really practice. Perhaps she attended mass every now and then or went to church with my father every other blue moon. But she was also very desperate and destitute in regards to the prospect of trying to raise three small children on her own.

So one night on a drunken impulse, half heartedly but perhaps with some spite for my father (who she thought was cheating on her), she took a bunch of pain pills to try to abort me. The raging sea was ever encroaching.

The next morning, my mother was still very pregnant. After this she succumbed to her basic motherly instincts and decided that since I was still alive, it must have been a sign from God to keep me.

However, when I was born into this world, Heath Christopher Goodman (or "The Beathers" as my mother affectionately called me), on May 10th 1967, the raging sea left a brutal scar.

I was born with multiple deformities. Some of my fingers hadn't fully formed and my feet were turned in from club foot. This was very likely from the pills she took during the developmental stages of the hands and feet. Doctors had confirmed that there was a high probability her abortion attempt could have caused the birth defects.

You see, I was ushered into this world with a death sentence already hanging over my head from within the womb of my mother. I was introduced to the raging sea before most children or adults begin experiencing any of the turmoil of the sea's hell. But in my Mama's belly, I hung on for dear life! I hung on with both hands and now I have lifetime scars to prove it! I was a "brand plucked from the fire". Though my mother, in a disconnected moment, did not want me, my Father in Heaven had a plan for me on this earth and for all eternity.

Dad, Mom Pregnant With
Me, Ally & Cully

My parent's faltering marriage seemed to improve after I was born. They managed to stick it out two more years, long enough to have another son, Sean David or "Seany". After he was born, the marriage fell completely apart. My mother became a single mother with four children. My father was in love at least fantasized about another woman, so he abandoned us like the rest of Mama's picks.

My mother was a very attractive woman, so she was never short of boyfriends or womanizing thugs who liked to use and abuse her. The 1960-70's sexual revolution pumped out a lot of single mothers and, of course, a lot of abortions too. If we as humanity were truly brutally honest about it, most abortions are not carried out because of a woman's need to save her life or dire situations, but only because of both men and women's unbridled lust to engage in irresponsible sex. Promiscuity, prostitution, infidelity and fornication (sex outside of marriage) is the real reason for 99% of abortions.

Perhaps there really is a reason why God absolutely forbids these behaviors... not because he wants to ruin our "fun" or "boss us around with holy commandments"... but because all these behaviors release the raging sea upon mankind and end up snuffing out the lives of precious babies. All because of sexual irresponsibility, comfort or inconvenience. Perhaps a loving God truly knows best and doesn't want us to have to experience the sea's hell. This is why God wants two souls (a male and female) to be fully committed to each other (life long marriage) before engaging in physical intimacy that produces precious children, to be raised by both a mother and a father. Otherwise we have a world full of unwanted, unloved children- killed, orphaned or struggling with one parent in the raging sea of life. God's holy ways makes perfect sense if you think about it.

Anyways, my mother seemed to attract the raunchiest of characters. I think the drug and "party" culture is only filled with narcissistic dudes that prey on weak, vulnerable women. My mother needed a man or men to take care of her as "Snow White and her four little dwarves". There was no way out of the cycle of poverty and drug culture for her. Unfortunately, even though she loved "her babies" and tried to take care of us as best she could, we were dragged along in the turbulent lifestyle of drugs, sex and Rock and Roll. The raging sea had swallowed her up and though she wanted better things for her four children, we were drowning in there, right along with her.

ECHO: ASHES FOR BEAUTY

After Daddy and Mama divorced, we settled near Bloomington, Indiana. Mama had several boyfriends and they always ended up abusing us children and her. Drugs and drinking were the norm. So were drunken fights and bloody domestic violence against Mama. She seemed to always gravitate towards men who were macho and loved to use women as punching bags. How Mama survived, I really don't know. I think Mama needed a man, any man to help her survive the raging sea. Instead, they became the raging sea or an ugly sea monster within it.

As toddlers and young children, we were living in constant uncertainty and fear. Mama loved her children dearly and we loved her, but she was a real mess. She was a liberal hippie girl who was caught up in the false messiahs of drugs and alcohol, with four munchkin children clinging to her hip.

I remember, on several occasions, falling asleep in my warm, soft bed and waking up alone or with Seany (or all of us children) in the cold back seat of a broken down sedan, in the dark. Looking out the darkened windows, I would see giant rocks all around the car. It was super scary for a 4 and 5 year old! Soon enough, Mama would come check on her screaming, hysterical children. She was drinking, partying and going skinny dipping with her friends after midnight in a local quarry hole.

Mama finally hooked a young man 14 years her junior, Marvin. He was barely an adult when she started dating him. Marvin was a good ol' boy from the backwoods of Indiana. Marvin was also a party animal, another macho dude who was compelled to beat up Mama, especially when he was drinking. She knew how to pick 'em, that's for sure!

Drugs, marijuana, beer and whiskey were all part of the regular diet between welfare checks for Mama and

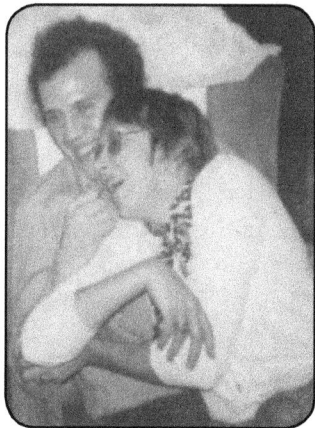

*Mom & Marvin
Happy & Stoned*

37

Marvin as they tried to brave the raging sea, stoned and drunk together. Unfortunately, the raging sea only rages more when you introduce elements that screw up your mind and your better judgements.

Mama wanted to become a psychologist but she ended up needing one every so often.

Mama was an avid reader and had a very high IQ. That is, except when she was drinking alcohol, or what I like to call "stupid juice", which is scientifically proven to dumb you down the more and more you consume it. Comprehension and motor skills are slowly diminished. Drink one or two beers and you're okay, maybe. Drink two or three and you're in your 20's. Drink four or five and you're a teenager. Drink six or seven and you're about 10 years old. Drink eight or nine and you're comprehending like a 5 year old. It's about the same with your motor skills. Drink a whole twelve pack and you're a slobbering, crawling newborn baby who craps and vomits everywhere.

As a toddler myself back then, I hung around a lot of "5 year old" and "newborn" grownups. The scary thing about it is they thought they could drive cars, hold on to jobs and manage families.

One of my earliest, most vivid recollections of my life with Mama and Marvin was a time when the raging sea viciously struck out and almost killed Mama, whom I loved with all my heart. I must have been 5 or 6 years old when Marvin came home drunk one night and beat Mama to a bloody pulp, literally almost to death, in a fit of a drunken rage.

I remember it so well because it made a deep impression of the raging sea in my soul that still echoes to this day. When Marvin came in, I had been sitting at the kitchen table playing with my toys.

I could tell he had a very angry expression on his face as he barreled passed me. He began slapping, fist punching and beating on my mother in the living room. I wanted to help my mother but I was so afraid of Marvin. I ran under the kitchen table and hid from him. Marvin's father came in and took him off of her. The next thing I saw was "Grampa" tumbling around with Marvin on a bed, trying to calm him down. My mother was rushed to the hospital with multiple broken bones in her jaw. She had to remain in the hospital, only sipping food through a straw for a good while.

From that night until I was in my late twenties, even after I had become a Christian, I held on to a little boy's guilt and shame. You see, in my little boy brain back then, I thought that if I had just smiled and said, "Hi Marvin," when he first came in, he would have then smiled back and been made happy. He would not have hit my Mama at all. I actually blamed myself for my mother almost being killed and put in the hospital that night. The raging sea had left a scar within my psyche that only by a miracle could later heal. Only after God took me and shook me one day, long after my conversion, did I realize that I even held such guilt and shame deep in the recesses of my heart... a guilt and shame that was misappropriated to my soul by devils, who sought to keep me in chains at the bottom of a raging sea. But God spoke through the darkness as a lighthouse beaming through the crashing waves. Like a huge burden falling off my heart, I remember the freedom from that fraudulent boyhood guilt and shame. Another chain had fallen and I thrust upwards and out of that raging sea which had held me prisoner.

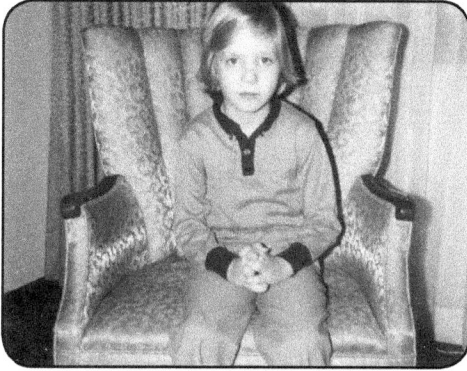

About The Time Mama Was Put In The Hospital

The devil still works the same dark devices in his shop of horrors with so many of us. Many hold on to similar types of misappropriated guilt and shame from a raging sea, in which they had no control over the evil that was perpetrated upon them or others. Perhaps it was a sexual assault or a domestic violence incident as well. Perhaps it was a parental divorce or giant betrayal by a friend or family member.

Whatever it was, whatever the guilt and shame you hold on to, Papa God speaks to you right now, today, as He did me that day when I was set free- "Your guilt and shame must not continue echoing in your heart and mind! Let it go, my beautiful child! It was never yours to hold on to! You were not the culprit. You were the victim! It was not your fault! It was someone else's selfishness and sin thrust upon you. You are not guilty! Now, please, my child, I want you to trade your ashes for My beauty. Trade your shame for My innocence and glory. I love you... be set free from the darkness that holds you down and condemns you!"

ECHO: DADDY'S BOYS, THE PICKLE KIDS

The pickel kids at Devil's
Hopyard
July 73
To Heath
as the air turns cold
The summer memories
Of sunday pichnics,
a splash in the lake
The ferry to the castle
And watching the rocks
Where the sea comes to break
Have lived in my mind
As happy times do
That neaver grow old.

Your Dad

The summer after Mama was hospitalized, Seany and I, just a toddler and a kindergartener went for a visit to Daddy's home in Chester, Connecticut. It was like a breath of fresh air to be away from the drinking, drugs and domestic violence. Daddy was somewhat reforming and no longer lived in that culture. We loved Mama but her erratic and loose hippy lifestyle made our little hearts fearful.

Daddy was so good to us that summer. He took us camping, fishing and "adventure climbing" at Devil's Hopyard, a beautiful, natural reserve with rivers and waterfalls there in Connecticut. We roasted hot dogs and marshmallows on an open campfire. Daddy would tickle us and tell us silly stories of him riding his motorcycle through Europe with a motorcycle gang and all the adventures and mishaps he had along the way. I know he embellished his stories to make them entertaining to us.

Daddy was a burly, short but stout man, with a flowing beard and mustache that sometimes made him resemble a "Wolfman". We loved his beard, what he called his "winter fur".

We loved playing with his Old English Sheepdog mutt, Shoddie. She was gray with curly locks that covered her whole face and eyes.

We went to see fireworks and a memorable July 4th parade in Essex, not far from Chester. Seany and I took turns sitting on Daddy's shoulders to watch the parade from an elevated viewpoint. Even though Daddy seemed to get tired more easily from his severe diabetes, this visit, he didn't show it often.

Playing Cards With Daddy

Back then, Daddy was a mix of bear hugs, fun and goofiness. He kept us in line, but he was not overbearing or brutal to us at that time. He was much more conservative in his perspectives on discipling children, having come from a prim and proper Christian home. This is one reason Mama had fought so much with him when they were together. Mama, didn't believe in spanking or teaching etiquette or self control at all. I am not sure how my parents even met, married and stayed together as long as they did with such diametrically opposing views and values. It was like Ms. Downright Liberal and Mr. Wayward Conservative fell in love over a beer and a joint? The 60's and 70's was a really crazy time I guess. Of course, we didn't have such a circus media as we do today, hyping up everything to turn everyone against everyone either. Conservatives and liberals were more tolerant of one another back then.

Anyways, Daddy also took us to Cedar Lake, which was within walking distance to his house in Chester. It was a beautiful, quaint lake that was shared by the little Chester community. We went on his sailboat and sailed on the lake a few times that summer. I loved it. We

42

would also fish off the little Cedar Lake pier. Seany fell in once. Just plopped himself into the water and began to sink. Daddy just extended his foot out and Seany grabbed on and was saved from drowning that day.

We would also go swimming at the little beach area. Daddy taught us how to skip rocks on the lake too. Daddy seemed to be a pro at it, while Seany and I managed to maybe skip a rock once or twice before it clunked to the bottom.

Sometimes Daddy would get silly and goofy when he was alone with us. One morning, he came into the breakfast table with half of his beard and mustache fully shaved only on one side. Seany and I looked at him and knew something was off about his looks but couldn't pinpoint it at first. Daddy mused and chuckled at us as we finally realized what he had done. Another time, Daddy kept speaking to the overhead chandelier light in the living room to turn on and off with just his voice. In the early 1970's there was no technology to do this, so Seany and I thought Daddy had mystical powers. He finally let us in on his secret trick- he was pushing the light switch off and on with his elbow. We laughed and genuinely had fun with our father that summer. It seemed like a magical time, filled with so many wonderful memories.

Seany and I adored Daddy back then. We were Daddy's boys, the "Pickle Kids". Seany and I would always argue which one of us was sweet and which one of us was sour. Daddy was so good to us then.

This is why we started spilling the beans on how we lived with Mama and Marvin in the raging sea. We told him about the fighting and violence, the drinking and drugs. We shared with him about the time Mama went to the hospital. We told Daddy we wanted to live with him. We had been smitten by Daddy's seemingly fun and wonderful life in Connecticut. We didn't know then that Daddy had put on his best for us that summer... but deep down there was a hidden, dark sea raging within him too.

After a nasty battle, my father was given full custody of Seany and I, with the exception of Mama's summer time custody. We were then ripped from our weeping mother's arms in Indiana and went to live with our father in Connecticut.

We loved our mother dearly. Had we really known that custody with our father meant long separation from our mother, both Seany and I would have kept the raging sea of her life a secret.

As our new life started there in Connecticut, we were somewhat happy to live with Daddy... at first. He was seemingly a lifeboat from the raging sea of my mother and Marvin.

But we quickly found out that Daddy had a dark side, a very dark side. The honeymoon soon wore off between "Daddy and his boys". Daddy started losing his temper more frequently. Soon we were smacked upside the head and screamed at constantly.

After a while, we were flinching and fleeing from our father's presence all the time.

His punishments became harsher and harsher. One of the first harsh punishments was torturous! We had to stand in a corner for what seemed like hours, balancing ourselves on one leg. If we used our other leg for support or just gave out, we were whipped with a belt and slapped around more.

This punishment was all because we dared to mock a ballerina on TV by saying, "Oh that looks easy."

Daddy became twisted and taunting in his discipline of us.

On one particular occasion, I can remember the day when the raging sea roared its ugly head. I felt like I had died or something died in me.

I was in the little kitchen in our house there in Chester. I saw a stick of butter on the stove. It was still kind of hardened from being in the fridge. Being the little boy that I was, I had what I thought was an ingenious plan to soften the butter and be able to enjoy it's buttery deliciousness. I pushed the little empty metal toaster down, putting the stick of butter up to the sides of the toaster to melt it. I soon began enjoying the melted butter by swiping my hand to catch the drippings and then lick it off my little stubby fingers. I was thoroughly enjoying my buttery fingers when Daddy came into the kitchen from outside. I saw the look in his eyes as he surveyed the buttery mess all over the toaster and countertop. I knew I was in deep trouble. Daddy screamed, "What are you doing?"

"Daddy, I was..." Before I could say anything else or try to "butter him up" with a great excuse, I saw out of the corner of my eye, my father grabbing the nearest object he could get his hands on... which unfortunately happened to be a cast iron skillet! Bam! A slam on my head and it was then like a movie script out scene- "fade rapidly to black".

I went out cold.

I just remember waking up on the top of my bunkbed in our bedroom. Seany was on the bottom bunk being consoled by my father. Although I could not see him from the top bunk, I heard him crying and asking my daddy, "Is Heathy going to die?"

"No, he is just sleeping. He will wake up soon," my father dolefully replied.

I just remember thinking that perhaps I did die and came back to life. At any rate, I was all right. Or was I? I don't think I was "all right" after that, as I did lose much of my admiration for my father and replaced it with nothing but fear and dread.

Don't get me wrong, I still loved my father... just not with great innocence or trust as before.

I truly believe this was when the raging sea began to agitate within me. Before this, the raging sea was somewhat an outward struggle but the innocence of childhood still held it at bay somewhat. The sea's hell was a turmoil contained in others which would slightly spill upon my childhood. However, being slammed out cold with a frying pan by my own father took the turmoil inwardly to the deepest part of my soul.

My father could have killed me that day. All it takes is one wrong angry swoop of a fist or an object to cease the life of another. How many people are confined to a jailhouse almost their entire lives all because of one stupid, senseless act of passion, one angry, undisciplined, even trivial seeming gesture? Most domestic violence cases that end up as murders are passionate accidents from a loved one, all because of a quick rash of anger and bad judgment. So many severed, broken families, crashing upon the rocks of a raging sea.

In the end, I was not dead but my relationship with my father had just taken a severe blow... and he had successfully transferred by way of an iron skillet, his raging sea to me.

45

A year or so went by and soon my father remarried. He found a wife from the Philippines. Her name was Josie. We immediately liked her and inwardly hoped that she would bring some calm to the raging sea in my father. As for the honeymoon period, she did seem to bring some stability to a lonely, ragamuffin Dad and his two ragamuffin sons. She was a little awkward with our culture and her heavy foreign accent made her hard to understand many times for the first few years. We liked her cooking well enough until we seemed to eat rice every single day. We would yearn for macaroni and cheese.

However, soon my father's raging sea could not be contained and he began abusing Josie as well. He gave her a few eye shiners, bumps and bruises.

I wish my brother and I could assume a righteous posture here and say that we defended our new step-mother and did not want to see her also screamed at, beat up or terrorized by Daddy's angry, psychotic moments.

However, if you kick a dog over and over again, soon his nature is weakened and he comes to bite his abusive master. The same can be said about children who are consistently abused. After a while, my brother and I were sort of glad that Josie "shared" in our suffering. We actually saw Josie as the "third man to take a beating" while the two of us licked and mended our own wounds. If Daddy focused his raging sea at Josie and not us, then so be it.

Unfortunately, as the saying goes, "abused people abuse people". Josie became embittered as well. Soon enough she was running after Seany and I with broomsticks, and breaking hair brushes over our thick skulls. So much for the "third man shared suffering" idea, now it was two adult raging seas against the wimpy, rascal boys.

Our great move to Rockville, Connecticut would seem to be a sweet change of scenery with a lovely, lonely house on a long, winding hilltop surrounded entirely by forest. No neighbors in sight. Perhaps the raging sea wouldn't follow us there. But alas, the raging sea is never bound by outward circumstances but gushes out from inward places. No amount of tranquil atmosphere can calm the raging sea within a man. The raging sea originates in the tumultuous soul and can only terminate there as well.

Now that we were hidden on a hilltop, within a few years things went from bearable to downright hairy-scary. Daddy was clearly struggling to contain the raging sea within him, as there were truly good moments and truly horrific moments. One day, we might find relief as Daddy cheerfully took us fishing on a beautiful sun shiny day. The next day, we might be the ones strung up to be skinned alive in the rain, metaphorically speaking. Daddy was truly a Dr. Jekyll/Mr Hyde sort of guy. We just never knew when, where or how he would become unhinged... except we knew the secret that raisins or a bit of honey sometimes had the power to calm the raging sea in him. Raisins would stabilize his blood sugar and bring him back from the brink of being Jack Nicholson in The Shining. Thank God for Sun-Maid raisins- how many times we were saved from certain death by that wholesome snack, only God knows.

Oh, by no means were my brother Seany or I saintly or sweet innocent kids as we grew older. The raging sea had taken its toll on us. We were pretty ornery and full of our own tempests and temptations. But we were still just a couple of raggedy boys trying to survive the sea's hell without drowning.

Seany and I were more than brothers. We were like wounded sailors on a beaten, tattered vessel trying to brave the raging seas all around us. Mama was the mother ship, and our other siblings lived a thousand miles away, so we truly felt like it was the world versus Seany and I. We had no one else but each other to weather the storms. As the older brother, I did at times bind up the wounds of my brother. But sad to say, I also abused my little brother. Many times I did protect him, but also at times when I was afraid and cowering, I used him as the scapegoat, the patsy.

I let him take the blame for things and I also let him take the beating.

But to be fair to my psyche as a child, I did feel guilty for this, but I truly thought Seany was more able to take it because he was younger. I reasoned that Daddy didn't hit him as hard as me. I didn't realize that being two years younger than me, that the abuse might impact him more physically and psychologically. I hadn't read any psychology books back then.

ECHO: BARRELS OF FUN

Yet in the raging sea of my childhood, I can remember some good times, some silly times. Some even with Daddy, but his anger and darkness would overshadow any warm light that he gave off at times. Most of my fond childhood memories were with my little brother Seany.

Me & Seany

There were moments when my brother Seany might have thought I was out to get him too. Some of the things we did as ragamuffin siblings we would later come to truly laugh out loud about. I truly never wanted to hurt my brother maliciously, but some of the things we did together might not appear that way. As a big brother trying to figure out the world, I would use Seany as my beta test subject for "experiments gone awry". Seany was my lab rat. I knew there were risks involved in exploring what was fun and what was not so fun, thus I chose to minimize those risks by utilizing my kid brother.

For instance, one day we were playing in the forest around our house and stumbled upon an empty 55 gallon rusty, old, metal barrel... on top of our very steep hill. Uh oh? Yeah, uh oh.

"Seany look, we can have fun with this barrel!" I happily said. "We can get in it and roll down the hill. It will be so much fun!" Now honestly, I genuinely reasoned in my little boy brain that it would be fun. Of course, having never rolled down a very long, steep hill in a 55 gallon barrel drum, it was just a theory I had. I knew that we would need to test it out. Being that Seany believed and did pretty much anything I told him, I sincerely wanted to have a thrill ride with this barrel. I promptly convinced Seany that I was going to let him be the first to have the incredible, thrilling fun of rolling down a 500 foot steep embankment in a rusty old metal barrel.

"It will be like riding on a ride at the county fair!" I encouraged him profusely, as he did look a little hesitant and doubtful at the prospect.

"You promise it's going to be fun?" Seany asked with the most trusting, puppy dog eyes.

"I promise Seany... and after you do it, it will be my turn!" I confidently asserted with the truest of intentions.

"Okay, Heathy."

Having the proper "big brother" worship, Seany complied as he let me place him into the "ready to launch" position at the top of the steep hill.

"It's going to be okay," I smiled wide as Seany's face seemed a little too apprehensive. Then with one great thrust of my two scraggly arms, I launched the barrel down the hill and let the "good times roll" and "barrels of fun" begin... or so I thought.

As the barrel rolled down the hill, I heard Seany moaning and grunting in a choppy sort of way as it spun ever faster down the incline. I then had a flash of a thought. "Maybe, it wasn't going to be as fun as I anticipated."

The barrel continued to roll until it abruptly stopped from a tree stump that was in its path at the bottom of the hill.

Now how was I to know that Seany's scrawny little body would tumble and bang around inside the 55 gallon drum until enough spin and speed caused centrifugal forces to make Seany become one with the barrel?

Not having studied the laws of physics or inertia or centrifugal forces, I had truly been oblivious to the possibility that rolling down a hill in a large metal canister in excess of 30 miles an hour might not be so thrilling after all. As a matter of fact, I actually had this exact epiphany as Seany crawled his way out of the barrel, crying and extremely dizzy. Seany could hardly stand up. His head was spinning, and he was weeping his eyes out with disorientation, disappointment and disillusionment.

I started down the hill to make sure he was going to be alright when I heard him start crying with loud moans over and over again. "It's your turn Heathy. It's your turn!"

Of course, I had to do what all good big brothers must do in situations like this. I had to somehow distract Seany from my promise to roll down the hill too, and try to redirect his great desire for me to share in the "fun". "Let's do something completely different now, like playing cops and robbers or cowboys and indians. Let's go play something else Seany," I lovingly but firmly redirected.

Big brother worship finally kicked in and Seany responded, "Okay, let's play something else," as he wiped the remaining tears from his dilated eyes.

I wish now that my brother and I would have learned our lessons on silly things like that. Unfortunately, I used Seany as a lab rat other times as well. Like the "fun" of of spinning around in an electric clothes dryer once. Seany relived that "barrels of fun" moment. Another time, it was the "fun" of putting a commercial staple gun up to the thick skin at the bottom of Seany's foot and pulling the trigger. "It won't hurt. It will be fun," I always assured him, not knowing the real outcome.

Sometimes however, I know that I wasn't the only culpable factor in Seany being a lab rat and bearing the brunt of an experiment gone wrong. Like one time when we were playing with matches in the backyard. Our father had an old rusted motorcycle that just leaned up against the house. I honestly wondered what would happen if we threw a lit match into the old gas tank.

Well, of course I convinced Seany it would be "fun" to see what would happen. Yes, I did open the gas tank and I did give him the lighted match to throw in it. However, in all sincerity, I did not tell him to stick his face over the the opening of the gas tank to peer down inside. He did that all by himself.

So when the very little gas and fumes exploded in a great whooshing moment, my brother's eyebrows were almost completely singed off his face, in typical Bugs Bunny cartoon fashion. He also had black soot that he had to wash off his face.

Later that evening, at suppertime, Daddy looked suspiciously at Seany and a bit frustrated, but he couldn't quite put his finger on what made Seany look a little odd that day. Nonetheless, we kept that incident a secret. Most of our "fun" was kept a secret from Daddy.

I know many would say I was a cruel brother and I can't deny that I was at times mischievous, but I sincerely thought all these things might be "fun". I clearly remember thinking, "Seany is gonna have a great time!"

Yet, scattered across these defining moments of boyish adventure and intrigue, my brother and I used our imaginations to live and play like most normal boys do. Well, perhaps even a bit more, because when we escaped to the woods to play pirates or adventurers, we forgot about the the raging sea at home. The raging sea that was building up within us would become almost non-existent in these play times. When we were cowboys, we were cowboys, when we were Grizzly Adams surviving the wilderness, we were Grizzly Adams. Perhaps we didn't transcend the raging sea, but we were able to break free of it's hostile undercurrent in the brief moments of our childish imaginations.

I don't think I ever really intentionally wanted to hurt my little brother, or be the firebrand that brought more of the raging sea to him. It was more like the raging sea in me spilling over into him. Yet many times what seems abusive and unloving from an outsider's viewpoint, also might just be ragamuffin boys being ragamuffin boys.

You know, I never did roll down that hill in that barrel or get in the clothes dryer, or staple a big staple in my own foot. I learned my lessons by learning from Seany's. It was brutal for him but beneficial to me. In all actuality, my little brother Seany might have thought that he was the needy one, leaning on me, his big brother for moral support (and "fun times" gone a bit awry). The truth is, I needed him just as much in those turbulent years with our destabilized father. He was my little bro and I thank God he braved the raging sea with me... even if it was sometimes a spinning sea for him. God help me, I didn't mean that! It's my orneriness still seeping through.

ECHO: LIKE FATHER, LIKE SON

In time, life with our father in Connecticut became like a madhouse prison for my brother and I. I can not begin to tell you all the abusive instances we were subjected to. Suffice it to say, Daddy used unconventional disciplinary measures on us that I wouldn't use on prisoners at Guantanamo Bay.

As an echo in the raging sea, sometimes we were denied our lunch and supper as punishments. One time we were grounded to our room and we had not eaten for a full day. So my brother and I actually smuggled dry dog food into our bedroom to eat. From then on, we actually developed a taste for dog food and would snack on it whenever we felt hungry. I would tell Seany, "Let's go out in the woods and play and stuff our pockets with dog food to snack on." Yes, in our hunger, we learned to bark at the raging sea.

Once on a Sunday morning, we were all getting ready for church. I think my father wanted to genuinely serve God and be a Christian. He just had a lot of demons on his back and didn't quite know how to get rid of them. Anyways, Daddy came to our room and smiled at me (sarcastically) telling me he had a surprise for me. He beckoned me to come with him. I didn't read his sarcasm and thought he really did have a surprise for me. I thought to myself, "What's the surprise? It's not my birthday. It's not any special day."

I went out to the back of the house with him to where the dog pen was. He promptly smiled again, grabbed ahold of my neck, pushed me to the ground and rubbed dog feces on me. "You want to go to church looking like dog *$@#%!, then here you go!" He then pinched my neck real hard and brought me inside and shoved me in my room. "You better change your drawers and be ready in a hurry."

I felt humiliated and worthless... or at least more worthless than his mutt dog that he would not even think to violently rub feces on.

My father truly had a sarcastic and sadistic streak in him to say the least. Many times he would taunt my brother and I with just ideas of how he was going to punish us. On one occasion, I can remember that my brother and I were in trouble for something we had done, to really set my Dad off. He took us into a butcher shop where we saw a butcher chopping up meat portions. In the car on the way home, he told us that he was going to chop us up into pieces, much like what we saw the butcher doing.

He never corrected his words or told us he was just being sarcastic. As impressionable boys, we took his words as gospel fact. All day long we really thought Daddy was going to chop us up into little bits. Our words go deep into the soul, especially words spoken over children who see adults as truth tellers.

However, Daddy didn't butcher us that day. He just whipped us with a belt. We had a sigh of relief and hoped he would forget about the butcher guy and his meat cleaver.

The raging sea within my father made him very cynical. Every time he spoke or acted in a way that brought forth the frothing anger, my own soul was flooded with the raging sea. This seeded the same type of anger and sarcasm in me. Like father, like son. I remember my father screaming at my little brother one day for some little accident. "Your brains are seeping out of your head!" He scolded Seany.

Seany was even more impressionable than me and when we were left alone he asked, "Heathy, is my brains seeping out of my head?" He looked to me for honest answers with baited breath. He set himself up with that question. I wish now I would have told him the truth from the beginning. Instead, I saw an opportunity to have some fun, so I milked it for what it was worth. "Yes, Seany, your brains are seeping out of your head. It is a blue mist coming out of your ears. You can't see it because only other people can see it! You're getting dumber and dumber by the second because of it." I teased him a good long bit until he started crying. Then I felt guilty enough to tell him the truth. "No Seany, your brains are not seeping out of your head." Our words are powerful and can either bring life or death, either calm a raging sea or create one. I learned to create them like my Daddy did.

ECHO: RUN AWAY FROM THE RAGING SEA

We ran away from home or I plotted our escape almost every month.

The first time Seany and I ran away was when we were still living in Chester, Connecticut. My father changed from the Daddy we adored to the Daddy we deplored. He became increasingly more abusive and taunted us with ideas of sending us away to a state boy's home. He even drove us to one on a rainy day and showed us the outside of the murky and morose buildings. He said he was very tempted to leave us there. We had visions of Nazi concentration camp type torture and confinement, so we tried to be good for Daddy as much as we could. But folly is bound up in the hearts of children, so we failed miserably. Thus, we decided it might be best to run away. Run away to the only warmth we knew existed in the known world- our hippy, dippy Mama, full of light and love and the smell of marijuana.

We had no plan, no map, no sense of direction or where we were going really. Me, at seven or eight years old, Seany at five or six, we planned to walk from Connecticut to Indiana. To walk all the way back into the loving arms of Mama. So with nothing but the clothes on our backs and maybe a snack from the cupboard, Seany and I set out on our great 1,000 mile journey.

Dad & Shoddie

We loved Shoddie. She was Daddy's Old English sheepdog, so we would take her along with us, of course. Or was she the little angel canine that God allowed to escort and protect us along the way? At any rate, we had walked about an hour or so around the road bordering Cedar Lake. That's when we saw Daddy's VW Bug in the far distance, barreling towards us. I immediately told Seany to hide with me under a giant drain pipe, down the embankment from the road. We did this, thinking that Daddy would just drive on by and we could continue our trek to Indiana.

However, we forgot one thing. Shoddie, being the wonderful dog she was, stood at the side of the road like a giant lighthouse beacon, loudly blaring out, "Heath and Sean are right here!" As much as we beckoned and shouted for Shoddie to come down the embankment to the drain pipe with us, she just stood there, so cute with her shaggy gray hair covering her eyes. Of course, our father found us and we went back home with him that day. I am not sure he even knew we were "running away". If I remember correctly, we played it off as if we had just gone "exploring".

Another memorable time we ran away, we decided that we would bum enough change from people to catch a bus from one city to another until we made it to Indiana. We managed to get enough money and take the first bus from Rockville to the capital city of Hartford, Connecticut. Once we got to the big city, we were totally disoriented in the concrete jungles of downtown Hartford. We tried to bum enough money for another bus but it was getting dark. Also, we didn't even know which bus to take next or to what city. On top of this, we were getting very hungry. Finally, it was completely dark. We had nowhere to go so we sat on a covered bus bench near the road. The darkness swallowed us up there. Both Seany and I were starting to get scared and super hungry. I think we managed to scrape up enough change to buy a little snack item at a little storefront, but it was hardly enough for two hungry boys. We settled in for the night at the covered bus bench, laying our heads down on the cold concrete slab in the middle of the city. We thought we would sleep until morning and then resume our bumming for change. As we lay there in downtown Hartford, in the late 1970's, the world was very much different than it is today. Yes, there were evil people and sexual criminals back then, but not as prolific as the age of the internet and spiraling porn addictions, pumping out pervs and predators off a factory line in a lawless generation.

So even though we were so scared, not knowing where or how we would manage in the unfamiliar world around us, we still felt that being on the "father ship" was more terrifying than braving the raging sea in a raggedy boat full of holes and uncertainty.

We stayed put and began to get drowsy. It was surely after

midnight when a police patrol car drove up to the side of the curb. An officer looked over to see two scrawny boys curled up on a bus bench.

He looked straight into my drowsy eyes. The adrenaline of seeing the police woke me up. The cop beckoned me to come over to his patrol car.

"Son, what are you all doing out here at this time of night?"

"We're waiting to take a bus to go home," I said, trying to compose myself.

"At this time of night? There's no busses running now." The cop stared me down.

"Our mom is going to pick us up in just a little bit." I quickly responded.

The police officer started looking skeptically at me.

"Son, what is your name?"

At this point, I didn't want to give him my real name, so I made one up on the spot in the heat of the interrogation. "My name is Billy."

"Billy What? What's your full name"

"Um, Um, Billy Filamagaglahumpadaposchink"

The policeman squinted his eyes. "What did you say your last name was son?"

I panicked because I instantly forgot what name I had made up. Imagine that. "My name is Billy Hopadnartaquarkashnoo."

At this point, the police officer was not buying what I was selling.

"Billy, why don't you get your kid brother and hop in the back of the patrol car for me."

We rode down to the police station where they continued to press me and Seany for our real names. Several times we tried to give them fake names but we were lousy, hungry, tired, drowsy liars.

Finally, either the police found out our real names through their network or one of us broke down and confessed. They were not impressed with our master plan to bum quarters and take bus rides all the way to Indiana. Our Daddy came and picked us up from downtown Hartford and we had to go back to braving the raging sea on the "father ship".

Another time we ran away, we ran away during a cold harsh blizzard in the dead of winter. Not being the sharpest tool in the shed,

I surmised that one magical sleeping bag for the both of us would be plenty warm enough to sleep in as shelter from the raging sea.

Seany and I had gotten in trouble for something that I don't even remember and our father promised punishment in the morning. Well, never "promise" punishment to your children because it's not a promise to them, okay? It's a threat against their tiny butts, a threat against their persons. Especially if you happen to have a pinch of sadistic anger in you.

So instead of wondering and fearing what Daddy was going to do to us, I figured running away in the wet, snowy, freezing weather was a better option.

But I did have a great plan this time. I really did. Thanks to episodes of Grizzly Adams.

This time we would hike down the backside of the mountain (more like giant hilltop) that we lived on, with a sled to carry our stuff. We would sleigh ride and hike all the way to Indiana, over 1,000 miles away with a few sandwiches and snacks we packed. Oh what fun we would have on a no horse open sleigh. We would scavenge for food, drink water from lakes, rivers and ponds. Maybe we'd even kill and eat a rabbit or something along the way... even though I didn't think to pack a knife or even know how to wield one really. "If Grizzly Adams can do it, so can we," I thought to myself.

We waited until Daddy thought we were in bed for the night and then OPERATION: SURVIVE A FREAKING BLIZZARD IN A MAGICAL SLEEPING BAG AND SLED went into effect.

We took the sleeping bag and the food we managed to snuggle. I also took a black sock full of quarters dimes, nickels and pennies, equalling less than twenty dollars or so. I thought it might help our trek across the frozen tundra of the New England landscape.

So along we went, in the darkness of night, in a forest on the backside of a quasi-mountain. Temperatures were dropping rapidly. We shuffled our way through the snow and howling winds. Our faces and hands became blistered from the biting cold in a matter of minutes. We must have traveled far, for we had gone nonstop for at least three or more hours, it seemed.

And then there was a valley clearing! We were leaving the

mountain and it felt like we might have gone halfway to Indiana already.

But then I slowly realized, "Something looks awfully familiar with this new place." Well, it wasn't new at all actually. I realized that what we thought was a long and weary trek that must have put us close to the border of Connecticut, or even the border of Indiana, was a total letdown. We had managed to brave the blistering blizzard around the mountain to the back of Rockville's main marketplace and my 6th grade school. It was my school that I walk within 30 minutes to every stinking morning, Monday through Friday.

"What the heck? How did we do that? How did we walk so far and end up so freaking close?"

These questions were going through my frostbitten head as we finally were forced to search for shelter from the falling snow. We found a giant pine tree that towered just behind the back of my school. Underneath the pine tree, we unraveled the magic sleeping bag. Both Seany and I managed to crawl into it to keep warm. We lay there shivering under the tree for a good couple hours thinking that at any moment we would warm up, fall asleep and magically be teleported to somewhere sun shiny and warm. Instead, reality had to spoil our dreams. Seany was looking at me with purple lips and puppy dog eyes saying how cold he was. Guilt set in, as I imagined that I would probably freeze my kid brother to death if we didn't take drastic measures soon. We got so cold and wet even underneath that great pine tree. So finally I told Seany, "Let's go home." Whatever the punishment would be, it was not yet a reality like the biting cold. We rolled up the not so magic sleeping bag which had failed us miserably and trekked a different way home.

We decided to take the short and easy way. Our delusion as "Grizzly Adams" and braving the wilderness elements had been shattered. The promise of a warm bed and an unknown punishment from Daddy was most appealing to our frozen extremities. As we "shiver-shuffled" to our home in the wee early morning hours, we saw the sun slightly peeping over the horizon, giving us hope that warmth was on its way. We found our beds and crashed within seconds of hitting the pillows. When we awoke, the sun was on full display but the snow still lingered on the land. Our father must have either forgotten about his promise to punish us or God had mercy on two pathetic ragamuffin boys that day, or both. We weren't punished by Daddy but perhaps our running away in a freezing snowfall across the wilderness was punishment enough. At any rate, this was one of those times that Daddy never knew we had even run away.

I wish we had learned our lesson about running away on the spur of the moment, but unfortunately I had not yet exhausted the "101 Really Stupid Ways to Run Away from Home" files in my little boy brain.

On another occasion, Daddy had given us bicycles for Christmas and this surely was positive brownie points for him. Of course, after the holidays, the raging sea would again show it's ugly, bony fingers and I was hatching a new plan for Seany and I to escape from its clutches.

Where other times we had miserably failed, this time I was sure we would succeed at running away because now we had... SHINY NEW BIKES!

So early one Saturday morning, we took off on our shiny new bikes for the great state of Indiana, where Mama lived. I figured we'd pedal the backroads from sunup to sundown. Within two or three days tops, we would be in the loving arms of Mama. I never thought to calculate the distance times the rate of speed in which we rode our bikes. I never even thought about the sheer physical energy required to ride a bike nonstop for several hours, let alone a whole day of pedaling up hills, around traffic and in the drizzling rain!

Nevertheless, we rode and rode and rode to who knows where or if we were actually going in the right direction at all. We didn't have a map. I was just going by my inner compass that shouted, "Away from the raging sea and towards Mama," which must be in the opposite direction... right? Maybe that way?

Seany got tired quicker, what a wimp. Why couldn't he keep up with the big boys like me?

Anyways, the rain and mud puddles became a real nuisance to us. Especially when cars would go by and splash mud and water all over us and our not so shiny new bikes anymore.

We managed to pedal from sunup to almost sundown. But then those pesky, meddling policemen found us weary and worn down, riding haphazardly in the twilight hour, in the rain, in the middle of ferocious evening traffic.

They must have had an APB (All Points Bulletin) on us already, because they straightway knew who we were and took us to the police station. Our father came and picked our tired little hineys up ... and our not so shiny new bikes. Another attempt at escaping the raging sea had failed... and we were so close, only 993 miles or more to go.

Well, there were many other not so clever attempts at running away, where I schemed a scheme to dream a dream but to no avail. However, one last attempt to run away was sometime not long after the incident with Daddy putting a rifle to our heads.

Our father, I'm sure, was weary of us running away and having to explain to authorities that there was "nothing here to see" "no raging sea of domestic violence or abuse going on". He must have been convincing them of the "harshness of a custody battle and how we being in the middle of it, wanted to see our mother". Never once did any authority ever question us about being abused or being unscrupulously afraid of our own father.

That is until we ran away for about three straight days... but we really didn't run away at all.

You see, anytime after we'd run away, our father would really try to do better and treat us well. Some "family normalcy" would manifest in our time with him then. So when he began digressing from Dr. Jekyll to Mr. Hyde, not only did we want to run away for a chance at making it to Indiana, but if we didn't succeed, Daddy would put on his best behavior for us. Dr. Jekyll would return with goodies and gumdrops for at least a few days.

So I had this brilliant, mastermind plan that we would run away from home, but still benefit from the necessary food and water we got from home. Instead of bumming for bus rides, trekking through a blizzard or pedaling to paradise, Seany and I would just hide in the upper loft of our newly built detached garage. In the evenings, we would break into our house and steal the necessary food and water supplies needed for each day. We would essentially be running away without the failed experiences of hunger, exhaustion, cold and pain associated with it. The only thing I really didn't think through was how that managed to get us any closer to Indiana and to our Mama. Perhaps if we just held out long enough, Star Trek's teleportation would be invented. "Scotty, beam us to Mama's home cause there are strange alien sea monsters trying to eat us here!"

My plan was that we would live in the upper loft of the garage, enjoying the fruits of our Daddy's labors without hammers being thrown at us, cast iron skillets knocking us out cold, going whole days without food, just snacking on dog food, or the whippings, or the rifles to our heads, or the angry shouting and slap-arounds.

So we snuck some food for the first day and went up into the upper loft.

Here is where Seany and I played uninterrupted with only our imaginations sending us on pirate adventures, jungle safaris and wilderness treks.

Here is where I would play with Seany's imagination and tell him the grandest stories. We did invent teleportation... at least in our minds.

One of my favorite imagination play times and Seany's too, was the "real" Invisible Alien Spaceship that was just above us, filled with clones of me with different personalities. You see, I wasn't really just Seany's brother. Because of my deformed fingers being different than everyone else's on earth, I was actually a member of this alien clone "funny fingers" society. I would be beamed up to the mother ship and hang out with all my clone brothers, while one of them would simultaneously be teleported down to hang out with Seany.

"Okay Seany, I'm going to be beamed up now. I'm not sure who's going to be beamed down so you'll just have to wait and see."

Seany would look delightedly at me, believing it was all for real.

I would straighten my arms parallel to my body, then close my eyes and begin making a beaming noise with my mouth.

"Eeeeeeeeeeeeeeeeeeeeen!"

I would open my eyes.

Seany would stare at me in amazement and then ask, "Who are you?"

"Hi, I'm Funny Bones! Ha Ha! I like to laugh and joke about."

I would laugh and tell jokes and try to make Seany laugh. Seany came to love Funny Bones as his favorite clone brother.

Sometimes I would beam down someone Seany didn't like.

"Eeeeeeeeeeeeeeeeeen!"

"Who are you?" he'd ask again.

"I'm Mr. Meanie! I don't like you at all!" I would then play like I was punching Seany and slap him around as a pathetic version of Daddy on low blood sugar. I didn't really hurt him too bad, but Seany definitely wanted me to beam him back up and beam someone else down, preferably "Funny Bones" or "Mr. Nice Guy".

There were other character clones like "Crybaby" and "Sadface" who had similar mopey, weepy personalities. There was "Angryman" who also reminded Seany too much of our reality. There was "Mr. No Fun" who was super serious all the time and a real party pooper. There was "Hiccups" who always had the hiccups and "Sneezy" who sneezed almost every time he spoke. "Giggles" was a lot like "Funny Bones" but pretty much only giggled, which got somewhat annoying to Seany.

Seany loved when I would beam up to the mother ship and he was able to hang out with all my clone brothers. Except he didn't like the fact that while he was meeting all these different clones down here on earth, I was up on the spaceship eating ice cream, cake and cookies, having a party with everyone else.

Poor Seany believed almost everything I told him, even some of the most outlandish doozies. I did wish I had really eaten ice cream and cake on an alien ship full of clone brothers though. Instead, I had to eventually beam back down to the reality of a raging sea around me.

Uh oh. I feel a Dad rant coming on.

Some professionals might discern my overactive imagination as escapism and childhood coping behaviors. They may say it was a self made protective bubble to deny myself the abusive reality around me. This may be close to some of the truth.

But I know why I constantly lived with Peter Pan in Neverland... it was my personal seashell protecting me in the raging sea.

Let me explain.

When a mollusk, snail or a conch is born into the raging sea, they are born as one of the most vulnerable life forms of the sea. They are basically soft and slimy tissued creatures who, without protection, would not be able to survive the raging sea for very long at all. However, the Creator who designed them put a mechanism within them that they would actually form around them a translucent exoskeletal frame. As they grew and endured the raging sea around them, this exoskeletal frame hardens and turns into a dense, strong seashell which serves to shelter them from the harsh environment of the sea. The hard shell almost completely envelops them and they are able to live out their life span as the seabed creatures they were destined to be.

We Form A <u>Seashell</u> To Protect Us From The <u>Sea's Hell</u>

Biological sciences have determined that the very structure of the seashell is in part a peripheral function overtly within their very DNA, and partly a symbiotic development from the turbulent sea environment that they must adapt to and endure.

Not all of these creatures who develop seashells are the same or develop the same sort of seashells. They come in so many different designs and features. Some are very spiral, others with rivets and spikes. But all serve the same purpose, to be the shelter that protects them within the raging sea. The conch shell is one of the most intriguing. It is very durable with an extremely crack or chip resistant shell. This shell is developed in natural design by layers of materials that crisscross in patterns to make it almost invincible to impact or breakage. The conch shell continues to add layer upon layer until it becomes one of the largest shells of the sea.

Likewise, myself, my brother, you yourself and of course every human being who ever existed develops our own seashell to shelter each of us from the raging sea. It may be a play on words that spells out the same, but we do indeed develop a seashell to survive the sea's hell.

As for myself and those of us who have received a lot of abuse and suffering as children or even as adults, our seashells tend to be of various shapes and sizes. Some build their seashells out of their introspective imaginations and go on to become some of the most creative artists, musicians, writers, speakers, etc., because the raging sea propelled them to retreat within an imaginative wonderland, which in turn allowed their creative energies to flow and expand. Yet, others resort to just consuming the creative life of someone else by escaping into books, movies and anything entertaining enough to keep them distracted from the raging sea, both from within and without. They actually are the crablike creatures of the sea, which find an empty seashell and make a shelter out of it. Bookworms, movie fiends and obsessed video gamers overly consumed in these things, or really just anyone who must escape into a virtual world, do so, to survive the reality of the raging sea around them.

Some folks create their seashell out of sex, drugs, alcohol and anything that can give them pleasure to counter the pain of the raging sea. Unfortunately, those things actually make the raging sea more turbulent and hellish. So the actual seashells that they develop become someone else's raging sea. One uses drug abuse to escape their pain while creating pain in others from that self same drug abuse.

Some pursue money and materialism as their shelter from the raging sea. Still others will pursue multiple relationships, religion, intellectualism or philosophical reasoning to shield them from the raging sea and/or to make sense of it.

We all inevitably develop some sort of seashell in our lives in order to try to survive the sea's hell. I can guarantee there is a high probability you have a seashell on your back right now. What it is or what social construct that it forms into varies, but the truth is, your seashell is a direct response from your sea's hell. Unfortunately, all these seashells end up washing up on the lonely shoreline of humanity, broken, uninhabited, destitute of all life. Seashells can never allow us to live forever or last forever in the raging sea. We just leave behind empty shells... If put to another's ear, it will only echo the sadness of our raging sea.

So anyways, back to my story of running away by staying put... Seany and I retreated into our imaginations and almost three days in the upper loft of the garage. We had to hide once and not make a sound when Daddy was searching for us. After the third day, however, we had run out of imagination, food and courage to sneak into the house to replenish. We decided it was time to go back to the house. When we came in, Daddy was actually sitting with a local forest ranger who had been out scouring the forest and lake reservoir below the mountain looking for us. The forest ranger saw us come in and our Daddy asked where we had been. We confessed to being no more than 50 yards away. After Daddy gave us a token scolding but was pleasant enough since the forest ranger was there, we were given something to eat. I remember the forest ranger looking over at us and at my father for a moment and then asking, "Why do you think it is that your sons keep running away from home?"

I don't remember Daddy's reply, but clearly he did not tell him anything about the raging sea.

ECHO: FROM ONE RAGING SEA TO ANOTHER

Although the sinister plot of wanting to kill Daddy seemed to diminish a little and we were also growing weary of trying to run away all the time, we still badly yearned to be with our mother.

Fortunately, in the summer of 1980 we were granted a short visit to see our mother in Indiana. We were only supposed to be their for several weeks and then return to Connecticut, to our father who still had full custody of us. Our mother once had summer custody, but kidnapped us and tried to relocate all her ragamuffins to Muncie, Indiana to live out our days with her there. We didn't get more than a few days enrolled in school with fake names when the police came knocking and took Mama away in handcuffs. Seany and I were escorted by our grandparents back to Connecticut.

Anyways, Daddy gave into Mama's plea to let us have a two week visit with her. After this summer visit was up, my brother and I reluctantly submitted as we were driven to the airport. We had such fond memories of the few weeks we had with our lovely Mama. We went exploring in the woods with our big brother Cully. We splashed and caught crawdads in a creek in Ellettsville. We played with our cousins Nunzio and Robbie in the trailer park. We loved every minute of our time in Indiana and we totally forgot about the raging sea back in Connecticut.

Sean, Cully & Me
Catching Crawdads

But a funny thing happened at the airport. I myself was morosely passive and very much surrendering to the fact that my brother and I would have to return to Connecticut, where we would definitely have to follow through with killing our father. If we wanted to ever live with our mother forever, we would have to go through with one of the dastardly plans I had thought of previously.

But Seany snapped like a rabid dog at that airport. He would not get on the plane. He screamed, held onto chairs, punched and bit everyone around him. The airport personnel just looked at my mother and said, "There's no way we can have this child who is in so much psychological duress on the plane. You will have to make other arrangements."

And that was that. As we drove back to Mama's trailer, I was exhilarated that my brother had gone off like a mad man at the airport. "Bravo Seany" I thought, "Why didn't I think of that?" We would be able to stay with our mother at least a few more days until who knows what would happen? My mother was scolding Seany outwardly and pathetically, but we knew deep down she was so happy to have us a little longer too.

A few days later, authorities showed up at Mama's door to escort us to transportation arrangements to enforce the custody situation. Seany and I scrambled to hide ourselves until they had left.

Another week or so later, our own father showed up at the doorstep of our mother's trailer.

Again, we scrambled and hid ourselves. I hid under my brother Cully's bed, panting and scared. I just hoped my father and the raging sea would go away and leave us alone.

My mother came in and told us that my father just wanted to talk with us and he promised that he would give us opportunity to stay longer.

"Come out from under the bed. He just wants to talk Heathy and Seany." Mama pleaded. Mama was a mess but she was trustworthy.

So, reluctantly, we both came out and went to our father, who then coerced us to get in the rental car and "take a little drive... just for a chat".

As we drove in the car, my father was somewhat subdued and trying to be as cheerful as he could. He began talking about our life in Connecticut and how he was going to change and be better towards us. He said John, our little brother needed us. He told us that we were not in trouble for resisting to return and that he understood our fears.

He then told us something that sent shockwaves of hope to our little darkened hearts. "But I am tired of the running away and constant

67

stress of knowing that you don't want to live with us, so if you choose to stay here in Indiana then I won't stop you."

"What, did I hear that correctly" I thought. "Did he just give us the option of living with Mama, the dream of our dreams and the only reason we ran away so very often?"

Yet in saying this, he was also trying to pull a slick one on us as he got on the freeway that headed towards the airport.

Immediately, we both began fearing the worst. We blurted out forcefully and most assuredly, "We want to stay with Mama! We want to stay in Indiana!"

As our father drove, I believe he began to sense the intensity of the raging sea within our hearts. He knew that it would be useless to try to get us to get on the plane with him. He knew that another "episode" would play out again at the airport. I am not sure exactly why he did it, but when we confronted him that he was going towards the airport, he almost immediately turned the car around. He could have screamed and threatened us in the car and got us so scared and docile that we might have returned to Connecticut with him on that plane. But I think he was tired of the raging sea in his own heart and in us. Deep down, he knew that he needed to give up the fight. Perhaps Josie had also rationalized with him that it was best that he let us go and let them start a fresh family with just John and Peter.

Whatever the reasoning, we had a sigh of relief when he pulled the car back up into Mama's driveway.

He gave us a choice and we chose to stay. He gave us a hug but it wasn't one of his "bear hugs". I could tell Daddy was visibly saddened that we did not choose to go back with him. He told us he loved us. I am sure he loved us as best he could with his conditions... but the greatest expression of his love that day was when he let us go.

Both Seany and I couldn't walk away fast enough from our father that afternoon. He pulled out of the driveway and then he was gone... and with that, the raging sea within us seemed to be diverted.

Seany and I were extremely exhilarated and it was perhaps the most joyous day in our childhood. Our dream to live with Mama had just now manifested! Though still unsure that it might be some sick joke from Daddy, we were genuinely happy and deeply apprehensive too. But for now, no more strictness and abuse. No more running away! We were going to stay in Indiana and leave the darkness of our father's madness! We were free!

Little did we realize, the pendulum that swings extremely to the right also swings extremely to the left. The raging sea didn't really leave us that day. It just took a drastically different dark form.

While Daddy was an abusive and sadistic disciplinarian, Mama was not a disciplinarian at all. Yes, abuse in the form of rigid law, no grace, no freedom, excessive punishment and pain is bad enough for a child. But abuse in the form of lackadaisical lawlessness, no borders or guidelines, no discipline or loving boundary limits may be even worse in many ways. As children, we may not have needed oppressive law and order, undue structure and obstacles to block us from being naturally creative and curiously intuitive. Yet we also definitely did not need unhinged freedom to do anything our our little immature hearts, full of folly, so desired.

Living with Mama was so freeing, so diametrically opposite from Daddy in almost every way. Free from what we thought were oppressive things like chores, church and curfews. Yeah, we were free alright, free to hobnob with drug party animals and shady characters of all types, to start smoking cigarettes, dipping tobacco, drinking alcohol, smoking marijuana, and experimenting with other drugs at age 12. We also continued to pursue our petty thievery skills, so that we might grow up to become jailbirds. Of course, our mother didn't outright condone any of these things for her children but this was her lifestyle. Her husband, our step dad Marvin, smoke, drank and even sold marijuana and other drugs. So it's hard to tell your kids "no" to elements that you have laying around the house everywhere. We had whiskey and pot parties, kegs of beer and bongs of Hashish. We had stray dogs, stray cats and stray humans partying, or having sex, or sleeping and vomiting all across our little mobile home trailer. It was so gloriously gross.

Now, the God of the Bible might have been a faint and hypocritical concept at my Daddy's home, but the god of hedonistic pleasure (whatever feels good, do it) was definitely worshipped at Mama's home. We also were introduced to much sexual, adult oriented entertainment and perversions of every type. Our raging sea went from church going, sadistic madness at our father's to lawlessness and total spiritual degradation at our mother's. The devils of the raging sea love when people live in extremes, whether to the right or to the left. So I escaped the conservative church going, overbearing (sometimes sadistic) Daddy to replace it with the liberal, anything goes, free spirited, hippy, lawless Mama. From one raging sea to another.

ECHO: TEXAS OR BUST

It was only one short semester of 7th grade in Ellettsville, Indiana when Mama and Marvin decided to make a giant leap of craziness to move the motley clan to Texas. Allyson, my sister and her boyfriend had been there. They had painted Texas as the land of opportunity with nothing but blue and warm sunny skies. It was winter break and we had packed up as much of our belongings as we could possibly fit in an old jalopy of a vehicle, piled high with furniture and luggage. Mama, Seany, myself along with my sister Ally, her boyfriend and all our cats and dogs would ride in the broken down car. Marvin and his friend Gibb would ride in the old raggedy van we also had. Cully would ride a broken down motorcycle. It was a real sight to see. Sort of reminded me of the Beverly Hillbillies song, "...so they loaded up their truck and they moved to Beverly... Hills that is..." Except we had little money and perhaps unseen devils slithering all over us. We were loaded down with lots of junk. Mama was making her big move to the Lone Star State.

It was already crazy enough but it went into overdrive insanity when Cully, my teenage big brother, with co-conspirators robbed a liquor store of a huge cache of hard liquor just before we were to launch off. I remember seeing tons of Vodka, Jack Daniels and a slew of bottled "Spirits" loaded down in our trunk as we started our journey to Texas.

What should have only taken a few short days, took over a week and half to make the trek. We were just a bunch of party animals, drinking, smoking weed, getting silly, stupid and angry, in that order. Sputtering down the highway, breaking down several times, getting totally lost, we lost cats and dogs along the way. I still find it hard to believe we ever made it to Texas alive. God was looking out for us even then in all our debauchery and dumbness. I think the raging sea was tossing us around, taunting us in our madness and mayhem.

Nevertheless, we somehow made it to the ginormous city

of Rising Star, Texas, population 339. When we looked around at all the tumbleweed and lack of storefronts and gas stations that we could pillage and rob, someone made the statement. "Is this really the promise land?" We scratched our scrawny, raggedy heads still reeling from truck stop hangovers and flat tire layovers.

We stayed in Rising Star for just a short time before we were forced a little south to a larger city, Brownwood, Texas, Population 24,000. Marvin and his friend Gibb found work as construction workers when the Heartland Mall was being built.

ECHO: THE SEAMONSTER RETURNS

Drug & Drunken Parties All The Time
Mama Was Becoming A Full Blown Alcoholic

In Brownwood, we settled in at several locations around the town. There I plunged deeper into the drug and alcohol crazed culture. I was was enrolled in Junior High and like most schools I attended, I felt as if I didn't fit in. I hated going to school almost as much as I hated staying sober. At 13, I was still picked on and made fun of in school for my deformed fingers. They called me "Funny Fingers" and bullied me quite a bit. As a typical teen, I did like girls a lot... but because I had such an awkward complex and low self esteem, I always felt clumsy, untoward and socially awkward around them.

Generally, the only time I felt confident or empowered was when I was buzzing from alcohol. Of course, my drunk confidence always turned into stupid mush talk so I never seemed to attract any teenie bopper girl for very long.

I ended up retreating into drugs, alcohol, fantasy and my imagination to push back against a growing loneliness and sadness in my soul. The raging sea was starting to swallow me up.

I developed a reading and writing obsession, thanks to my Mama. Even as a young, messed up hippy dude, I liked the idea of retreating into novels. Mama turned me on to the science fiction writer, Isaac Asimov and others. I would devour his thick novels in days as I lived in a world of fantasy and adventure, far away from the bitterness of the raging sea.

As time progressed, I digressed further and further into darkness and despair. Oh, most of my family were too busy in their own happily depraved states to even notice my spiral downwards. My mother became more and more hooked on Vodka and had her own demons to deal with. She hid bottles of vodka everywhere throughout the house. She seemed to be losing more and more control of her family as she soused her brains in stupid juice. She was slipping deeper and deeper into an unsustainable alcoholic addiction. My sister Ally, my brothers Seany and Cully were all in different stages of their own drug filled, marijuana smoke ring debauchery.

The more pot I smoked, the more beer I drank, the more drunken parties I attended, the more science fiction I read, the more I ended up feeling lonely, angry, worthless and without real purpose.

Something definitely was starting to unravel within my psyche and soul.

Depression is the result of a faithless, "God-is-dead" existence, lost with no purpose or compass to guide you. I began having deep sadness attacks, feelings of extreme emptiness with rain and low, gray clouds blotting out any sunshine to my soul.

We moved around Brownwood for a couple years until my mother and Marvin finally landed a house in Blanket, population 400, that we were actually going to buy. Imagine that, my hippie, drunken nomad Mama, finally settling down with a real mortgage! We had always rented so this was a real milestone.

When we first moved to Blanket, Texas, I thought we had moved to the boonies of boonies, where the only thing to do there was watch the turnips grow and hear the fluttering of cows going "moo moo" frolicking in the nearby pastures. I didn't like it and didn't want to be there. I actually rode to Brownwood everyday with some cowboy hicks to finish out my eighth grade year at Brownwood Junior High.

All I ever heard about Blanket was that the people were

all straight-laced "Rednecks" and "Kickers" (boot wearing rodeo loving cowboys). This, of course, didn't fit in with the long haired hippy drug culture.

I started attending Blanket High in 9th grade. I hated every minute of it. Being the only long-haired hippie with glaringly deformed hands among cowboy hats, jocks and rednecks, I had no friends whatsoever in the school. I only hung out a little with a scraggly tall guy with a shaved head, nick named "Bird". Bird was a little slow and somewhat of a misfit himself. His tallness, lanky walk and overall creepy appearance kept most everyone from socializing with him as well. He reminded me of a character you might see on the Addams family. I liked him though because he didn't thwart his nose upwards at me. He was down to earth, where I tended to hang out. For the longest time, I would eat by myself in the school lunchroom. Only Bird would pull up a chair and sit with the "finger freak" hippie.

It was around this time that weird, paranoid "panic attack" episodes began.

Marijuana is a drug that can seriously give you paranoia and restructure your brain to think crazy thoughts. It's not an innocent, non-harming drug. It seemed every time I would "get high" that my mind would go into this strange paranoia and loneliness state. I would obsess while buzzing, thinking that my mother was going to die, the only true person I felt loved me unconditionally.

The paranoia attacks got so bad that I started turning down joints being passed around or I would pretend to take a toke just to fit in. I still smoked it from time to time, but the paranoia was becoming a black hole in my raging sea so that I no longer craved it as much. Instead, I turned to drinking alcohol more profusely. I sometimes passed on the joint but doubled up on the beer. I would literally get drunk almost every weekend and go to school on Monday with a hangover. Yes, I tried to drown my sorrows in the raging sea with "Southern Comfort", only to get none.

I remember an incident about this time that showed me

how much darkness and bitterness was truly in my heart, how much of the raging sea had taken from my humanity.

Being lonely and having no friends, I really craved to fit in. So one Friday night, I went with Bird to a rodeo that was taking place near the Blanket school. I had never been to a rodeo. I was there minding my own business and kind of enjoying the cowboys being bucked off of violent bulls when I was suddenly approached by a gang of "kickers". I didn't know any of them. The main guy started mouthing off to me."What are you doing here at the rodeo, boy? Don't you know this ain't no place for you or your kind of hippy friends?"

He started getting up in my face trying to provoke me.

Quick rant: In today's world, this would amount to extreme bullying and "racism". The truth is, "racism" stripped of political correctness is just any hateful behavior anyone shows toward another human being. That's all. Simple really. No one should sit on a high horse and claim to be free from being a "racist". All humans possess the potential and propensity to hate. So everyone should stop virtue signaling by pointing fingers and feeling superior to each other in this regard. We all learn to hate just as we all can learn to love. A racist (or hater) can change to love again. Only people with political agendas and hypocritical, self righteous bony fingers will declare "once a racist always a racist". But people can change. The raging sea does produce hatred and "racism" but there is a way out. End of rant.

Anyways, the kicker dude became very threatening. I was not a fighter or a lover either. I was pretty much just trying to be a mellow stoner dude now, trying to fit in the world of straight-laced, prejudiced, churchgoing, one gallon hatters.

"The rodeo is not for freaks like you," the lead "kicker" snorted.

"Ok man, I'll go, dude." I was genuinely intimidated and wanted to just scoot out of there.

"I'm not a dude, you %&#$%!" the chewing tobacco dude screamed at me. Then, in what I could clearly see was an attempt to impress his "kicker" buddies and girlfriend, he swung his fist at me. He punched me in the face as I took the full force of it. He took several more swings at me until I was on the ground. He and some others kicked some dirt at me and laughingly left me in the parking lot, humiliated and bleeding.

Well, I walked just a little ways out of the parking lot before I started a full gallop towards my home. No, I wasn't running scared, I was running with a raging sea unleashed in me. I was so angry and determined to find Marvin's guns. I planned to go back there and blow that guys brains out along with all his bullcrap loving friends! No, I was not a lover or a fighter, but get me angry and I would release the full force of the raging sea on you, dude!

I ran into the house scouring all over to find Marvin's guns. Fortunately, I found none.

Cully, I And A Friend About The Time I Got Beat Up At The Rodeo

I then thought about using a knife of some sort. As I contemplated what this boot-stomping stranger did to me, I felt true evil, darkness and the full force of hatred envelope my soul. I was determined to go back to that rodeo and kill this guy and all of his friends, straightway. But I had to do it spectacularly so that no one would ever mess with this "finger freak" ever again!

So I ran to the garage to find any instruments of torture,

maiming or whatever I could use to impale the cowboy punk through his heart. I didn't find anything adequate to the spectacular. Until I stumbled over some kerosene and some of Mama's Christmas bulbs. Yeah! With these two things, I would make a fire bomb from Hell, where I would light a homemade wick and throw it at the dude, gleefully watching him "burn baby burn... Falalala, Merry Christmas in September!"

I just had to do some product research and development first. I had to test a few bombs on the side of the road near our house.

I spent an hour and a half making homemade bombs out of kerosene and Christmas bulbs. I tested them, lighting and throwing them on the road. However, the spectacular in my mind turned into a fizzle in reality. The kerosene didn't burst into a great fiery inferno on impact. A few times the fire went out and the bombs were completes duds. After trying to make a worthy bomb to completely destroy my enemies with fire, my anger languished and finally deflated altogether. I found out that I was not a good bomb maker. I also realized that I had some seriously deep, dark unresolved issues inside of me that no amount of marijuana could mellow out.

I went to bed that night wondering if I had found Marvin's guns or made a good bomb that I might have laid my head in a jail room cell that night, and somewhere, some farmer Joe would be burying his son the next morning. For the first time, I really saw the raging sea in me and I knew it was a scary, dark force that would eventually overpower me to do something really crazy and stupid. I learned to somewhat survive the raging sea around me, but how could I survive this ugly, raging sea within me? I thought the sea monster was gone now that I was identifying as a mellow stoner dude. But the sea monster raised his evil serpent head and I knew I was on a wicked path of destruction, drowning in a wicked sea.

Warning! "Dad Rant" just ahead-

Someone once penned, "I am a raging sea trapped inside

a raindrop". For me, and I suspect for everyone really, a more accurate phrase would probably be- "I am a raging sea trapped inside a teardrop, trapped inside another raging sea, trapped inside the tears of God." For I have both experienced a tempest within me to my own sadness and one all around me, as humanity crashes upon each other, inciting the anguish of the Almighty. If I examine the world through a microscope of just my own narcissism, I would only acknowledge the raging sea and subsequent teardrop inside of me. However, we are not islands unto ourselves. Clearly a monstrous raging sea exists in and all around every one of us. This is one reason I literally shook with so much festering bitterness and guilt that night, after I realized how deep and dark my heart truly was. I had actually planned to go on a mass murdering spree, all because some rodeo clown and his boot-licking thug boys banged me up a little and hurt my pride. I didn't just want to kill these people. I wanted to burn them alive and watch them suffer in torment! I realized that night that my heart was filled with a vileness and putrid scum that I had no remedy for. All I could do is further retreat into my marijuana, beer, sci-fi novels and rock and roll. I just wanted to be a mellow dude. I could only hope the fire breathing sea monster would never emerge again.

However, I found out that listening to Kansas's lyrics "All we are is dust in the wind" over and over again doesn't do anything for your self worth or your value of human life. Imagine that! Ozzy Osbourne's "I'm on the highway to Hell" didn't help either. I actually loved listening to music that beat up my psyche. It was my self inflicted punishment for being such a wicked soul. I allowed the spirits of darkness to cuddle and coddle my raging sea until I felt zombified enough to "carry on my wayward son".

You see, I was just this little speck of dust on another speck of dust called Earth, spinning around another speck called the sun, floating aimlessly in a vast galaxy that is also just a speck in a seemingly endless universe that is probably just a speck as well. My whole universe was most likely a neutron in an atom on a molecule on a skin cell of a wart on some puppy dog's nose in another reality. Science fiction and secular atheistic fantasy helped push this idea in me, this morbid, whacked out emptiness. So, not only did I have to battle a raging sea within and without, I also had to comprehend that my struggle was really a pathetically, worthless one.

Why even try to fight against the raging sea? Why struggle to survive from being swallowed up and drowned by the sea's hell? Why bother if "all we are is dust in the wind", if all humanity is just collective teardrops in an endless, lonely, offending raging sea? I began having extremely hopeless thoughts. I even began wondering if suicide might be the best way out of my ever increasing despairing reality. I was no one, going nowhere with no purpose. Just a deformed freak of nature living for the moment and then the moment was gone. Was this really all there was to life?

Did I believe in God at this time? Well, I made token references and gestures that some would interpret that I must have believed. But my gestures were mostly defiant fists raised in the air, cursing this invisible Daddy in the sky. Sort of like Bubba did on his shrimp boat, battling the raging sea in the movie "Forest Gump". A perfect iconic depiction of most of humanity's hostilities against God in the raging sea.

God was a concept like all the other concepts in my ragamuffin intellect. I could not prove He existed. Heck, I didn't even know if I really existed. Perhaps I was just a hologram TV program for some sadistic god's entertainment. My father was a taunting, sadistic fellow so perhaps this "heavenly father" was one too. I mean, why would He allow me to be born with deformed fingers and have a huge, cursed "mark of Cain" on my body for all to see and ridicule? I never paid attention to my hands until someone recoiled in horror at the sight of them.

I remember girls crying in elementary school because my hands slightly brushed by them and accidentally "touched" them. Was it my fault that I was born with two stubs that looked strikingly similar to Kermit The Frog's eyeballs? If there was a God, then I blamed Him for everything crappy about my life. He was blamed for my lack of girlfriends too.

I surmised that my life was just a bad accident that should have never happened. I was born into the raging sea without my consent and now I had to somehow overcome it? If I didn't overcome the sea's hell in this life, then I really had a raging sea of fiery Hell coming in the afterlife? "Thanks sadistic god, but no thanks. I didn't sign up for this toilet world, so You can't hold me accountable for what atrocities I might commit trying to keep from drowning in the flushing sea!"

The only way to hold darkness within our souls and not go crazy in our consciences with conviction, shame and guilt is to justify the evil within us, thus deceiving ourselves. So I justified my murderous tempest within, that almost killed the snuff dippin "Bubba" in a cowboy hat.

I prayed not for forgiveness or redemption for my murderous heart, but that if there was a God that He would keep people and circumstances from stirring up the raging sea within me. "If you don't want the sea monster to emerge, then God, don't allow anyone to ever hurt me again!" Yea, like that was going to happen in the raging sea... This was the only remedy there was... or so I thought.

ECHO: MY FATHER WAS DEAD TO ME

Seany and I had been back living with our mother for more than a year in Texas when a small package arrived in the mail. It was addressed to: Heath and Sean, the "Pickle Kids". We opened it up and it was a cassette tape and note from our father. The note was short and encouraged us to listen to the tape. Both Seany and I were a bit curious as to what was on the tape so we found a tape player. The heartfelt voice of our father came out of the speaker, something like this- "Heath and Sean, I just want you, my sons, to know what God has done in my life. He has really changed me into a new person. I want to ask for you both to really find it in your hearts to forgive me for the many times I mistreated and hurt you guys. I was really troubled back then. You are my "Pickle Kids" and always will be. I remember all the good times we had and I hope..." Click! I slammed the play button and turned off the tape player. I had heard enough and didn't really care to hear anymore. "Dad's trying to preach at us!" I said. For me there was no forgiveness. No reason to hear a full confession. My father was dead to me.

We also still feared he might be, in some way, trying to trick us into returning to his home. I took the cassette and began pulling out all the magnetic tape as the whole spool unwound and became a tangled mess in my hands. I started tearing the tape apart and had fun destroying it to shreds before throwing it in the trash. It gave me a sense of satisfaction that I was no longer under the control of my deranged father. He wanted me to forgive him... what a joke! How many times did I hear that before up in Connecticut after Daddy had gone to a church altar and prayed. Then later it was wham, a punch to my face or a rifle to my head! I didn't want his Christianity. I didn't care about him or his God really. My bitterness was still brooding, still bleeding in the undercurrent of the raging sea.

ECHO: DUMB AND DUMBEST, DARK AND DARKEST

Life in "Podunkville" Blanket, Texas, kept me keenly obsessed on finding new ways to numb my mind and heart to the harsh realities of being lost and wandering in the raging sea. I did finally manage to develop a sustained friendship with a fellow stoner dude named Eric. Eric would soon become my best friend. He was a natural, blue-eyed, long-haired, blonde and a chick magnet. I liked that my best friend could get chicks real easy and I was hoping some of that would rub off on me. But Eric went for the same girl I secretly had a crush on and she soon became his girlfriend. I guessed Eric just had more fingers than I did. The only benefit for me was that I got to see her more often. I could tell in her eyes that she like me too, but I was awkward enough. I would not dare put a wedge between Eric and I by trying to steal "his girl". Besides, I sabotaged pretty much all my attempts at finding true love at the ripe ol' age of fifteen. Every girl I ever liked, I thought in my heart, "She wouldn't want to be with me because of my deformed fingers. I'm not good enough for someone like that." I heard my father's taunts and ill words come to my mind. "You're a loser! You're good for nothing!"

Eric did attempt to "fix me up" with girls and I actually didn't sabotage one particular girl until she wanted to take the relationship to the "next level". Don't get me wrong, at fifteen and testosterone driven, I fancied the idea of a physical relationship with a pretty girl. It was just that I felt totally inadequate. My lack of confidence in myself, my looks, my personality, became a shining darkness on a hill. I know at fifteen many boys and girls are immature and unsure of themselves anyways. But I was like the super duper of teenage awkward dweebness. One thing that most girls, even to this day, will run fast and furious from, is a guy who has no confidence in himself. They're not attracted to dudes with self esteem issues who wallow in self doubt and self hatred... unless your Batman. I say "most" but there are strange girls out there who are attracted to unconfident guys. Oh, I tried to pretend to be macho and dude-like... but I always second guessed myself, and in the end sabotaged any chances of getting "the girl of my dreams"... which happened to be almost every girl I fancied as even semi-pretty at age 15.

Now Eric and I began hanging as a pack of stoner dudes with other guys like Jonny Boy who later died, having overdosed on drugs, and Fenton, the original "Gamer Boy" who spent almost every waking hour high on pot and playing on an Atari console.

Eric was always restless and ever expanding his desire to fulfill every hedonistic pleasure he could imagine. We generally followed him right off the cliff of insanity. He was the alpha male and I was just the number two guy in the pack. Eric and I hung together more and more until it seemed we were inseparable.

One day we were at Eric's house and had exhausted all our resources and ideas. We had no marijuana, no money for beer and had already jammed out way too much on AC/DC.

"Hey Heath, I know what we can do to get high. Do you wanna know?" Eric smiled.

"Yeah!!! How?" I responded.

"We can find some paint cans and huff on paint fumes. You ever do that?"

At first I thought he was joking but then he said it again. I could tell when Eric was having a humdinger idea.

"Isn't that dangerous? I've heard of people being hospitalized because of that."

"No, dude, it's not that bad. We're not going to huff it like stupid people do."

"But stupid people were made stupid from burning their brain cells like that." I thought out loud.

Eric jumped up off his bed. "Let's go out to the garage and see if we can find some."

I followed Eric because he was the 24/7 mobile party animal and I was the compliant sheep.

After a good while of trying to find some paint cans to no avail, Eric finally came to me with a gallon can of gasoline. "We can huff this instead."

"Gasoline! I don't know about that Eric," I said, as a very rare, stoner teenager trying to create a boundary line.

"Sure, man, it will be killer dude."

"You mean, it might kill us dude!" I patronized.

Eric pushed. "I've done it before and man what a rush... as a matter of fact, it's just like Rush!" (a common term back then for chemical substances like amyl-nitrites or "poppers", inhaled for a brief toxic stimulation to the brain).

"I'll even do it first!" Eric bravely chimed.

I watched Eric huff the gas fumes in his backyard for a minute or so. He then staggered back and almost to the ground. "Woah dude. It's crazy amazing man," he drooled almost incoherently.

I really didn't want to huff gas fumes, "but if Eric the stud muffin can do it, then I guess I could too," I thought, thoughtlessly.

I took the gas can and began huffing on it, allowing the toxic fumes to invade my nostrils and rip up into my lung cavities, destroying precious capillaries and delicate sacks that are supposed to hold only oxygen. In just a short moment, my brain felt a sensation; it spiked into a burning rush and then I almost blacked completely out. I fell to the ground. My eyes were open but all I saw were sparkly sparks.

Eric came over to me. "Do you like it man? Do you?"

"No, dude not, not really Eric... no man." I mumbled as I stumbled around trying to come out of my disorientation.

Eric just laughed at me. He started huffing the gas can again. He must have been a veteran at it because he was actually enjoying killing off billions of brain cells in mere seconds.

"There is no way I am going to subject myself to that again," I thought, as I started to show signs of recovery. However, peer pressure and wanting to impress a fellow stoner kicked in. I huffed gasoline several times after that, just to make Eric feel like

I was truly a part of his Club Stupid.

After we lowered our IQs by 150 points and our capacity to learn anything quickly or fluently ever again, Eric finally got tired of the gasoline. We went back into his house and found some munchies. In his room, Eric began showing me his different, odd assortment of things when he suddenly perked up and pulled out a giant black book from his bookcase.

"Heath, do you want to be able to get any girl you want? Do you want to be able to get money and things, whatever you desire?"

"Yeah, sure I do. Why?"

"Because I know how!" Eric's eyes sparked with excitement.

I was a little skeptical at that statement because if he knew how to get anything like money or things, why in the world did we just huff gasoline instead of buy a mountain of pot to smoke?

"Okay how?" I said.

Eric handed me the giant black book. The title read "Real Black Magic Spells and Incantations".

"This book is full of spells that you can perform that really work. I've done it!" He flipped to a certain page. "See this spell? It's a spell to cast to get any girl you want. I did it and that's why I'm with Sandra right now!" Eric exclaimed with full persuasion.

When Eric showed me the title, I was just a little taken back by it, due to having been somewhat raised in church with my father in Connecticut. But I was oddly intrigued and Eric knew how to push the right button in me.

"You got Sandra by doing this spell?" I said curiously.

"Yes, that's how I got her. I followed this spell and sure enough it worked. I've done other ones too and they also worked. I've gotten money and even cigarettes from doing a spell." Eric was frothing.

"Really?" I was interested.

"Yes Heath, we can do some spells together if you want. The book also shows how to do astral projection, about leaving your body and traveling in the spiritual dimension, I've tried it... it's way crazy real." Eric spoke with unusual enthusiasm.

I knew about astral projection from reading sci-fi books. "I'd like to try astral projection to see if it's real," I injected.

That night we both read more about how to do astral projection. We laid on the floor to position ourselves as instructed. Eric and I independently experimented with it. As I lay there doing the prescribed breathing, posturing and meditation, I started to feel something within me begin to rise out of my chest cavity. I actually started to feel my soul separating from by body. I also felt a very dark presence. At that moment a fear gripped me and I felt a jolt inside my body. I suddenly jumped up and told Eric, "I felt something come over me man, and begin to lift me out of my body... but I don't think I'm quite ready to tether my soul to the netherworld."

I think Eric got bummed out as he had not experienced anything but perhaps headache withdrawals from earlier huffing gasoline fumes.

At any rate, this was a pivotal night where I could definitely feel a greater darkness come over my spirit. I knew deep down that I shouldn't be dabbling with the occult and black magic, but something appealed to me about having supernatural power to control my destiny and to bring to my life anything I wanted. Perhaps this is how I was to survive the raging sea. If there was a God, perhaps he was some old ornery goat of a dude who just wanted to keep me down and in the dumps. Perhaps the devil was the real cool dude after all.

So Eric was able to get me to fry my brains on gas fumes and fry my soul on black magic, introducing me to the worship of Satan, all in one night. Boy did I love Eric... I mean, isn't that what best friends are for? After all, the saying is true, "The company that we keep truly shows us what path we're on."

Eric ended up being kicked out of his mom's house and began to live with me in my room at my house. We dabbled in astral projection and black magic at other times, but I was not as whole heartedly ready to sell my soul outright to the devil.

I don't think it was because I had a tinge of the fear of God in me, as much as I had a God fearing set of grandparents and my father (who had become a real Christian), who I'm sure were bombarding heaven for me in their prayers.

Eric wanted to do blood rituals and all kinds of crazy stuff that I would not allow myself to do. He actually wrote a "love letter" to Satan, expressing his desire to be fully taken over to the dark side. He wanted me to join him in a Satanic blood pact but he was spiraling way to quickly towards true evil for me.

You see, I, like most people, wanted to take the slow train to Hell. None of this sacrificing babies or killing innocent people to grow in power with the demons. We like the sound of wickedness going "Chugga-chugga-choo-choo-here's-a-little-sin-just-for-you". Even though I was hesitant of Eric's fast pace into raw Satanism, I was nonetheless curious to see where it would take him. If I saw Eric begin to get the money, women and power he craved, perhaps I could be persuaded to ride in the fast lane too.

I began experimenting with even stronger drugs as the days went on. Yes Virginia, marijuana is a gateway drug, where you lower your inhibitions until you start experimenting with other drugs. It's a natural digression. Eric and I experimented with you name it. Insanely, we would pretty much smoke dried cow manure if we thought it would give us a buzz. We might have actually done that but my smoke filled memories are bit fuzzy there. Maybe Eric had told me that he had read or heard something about cow's poop and methane gas and how to get high on it. To Eric, if a random potential substance entered his peripheral temptation to smoke it, he would say, "What the !@#%$!, let's give it a shot."

Try not to laugh, but unfortunately, cow poop sniffing is a real thing... and can turn into an addiction. Teenagers out west have actually died from it! Seriously. No, seriously! Pleeeease, just say no... to cow poop!

Back then, Eric and I would randomly experiment with different plants and stuff to see if we could find the holy grail of the perfect substitute high "when stoners had no pot"... Yes, I followed him off this "dumb and dumber" cliff. I don't think we got high on bovine dung, just so that you know. If my memory serves me, we only thought about it before a sliver of intelligence kicked in.

Eric wanted to keep our smoking experiments just between the two of us, probably because smoking random plants or animal feces hadn't become trendy or cool yet. Thank God, no one ever suspected or even accused us of smoking stupid things like dried bovine dung. I am sure there are laws on the books about that. You know, if you say bovine dung really fast like it was one word, it does sound, perhaps, like an exotic oriental drug or something... bovinedung! "Yes, officer, I must confess. I smoked some oriental bovinedung in my bong." Okay, I 'll give it a rest. Sometimes the raging sea rages with laughter... and it's not laughing with you but at you.

We also experimented with some spices found in the cupboard, but all we got were headaches and Mama 's anger for emptying her spice cabinet. We finally quit experimenting. I just thank God we didn't accidentally smoke arsenic or poison ivy, or I might not be alive to roar with laughter at our dastardly dumb deeds.

I know I am presenting my drug and alcohol use as kinda light hearted here, but the truth is, it's funny only because we were so very stupid and lived to still laugh about it. To be honest, some of my friends aren't laughing in their graves right now. My friend Jonny Boy overdosed on drugs and died before he turned 18. Another acquaintance/friend, Shorty, was shot dead in a drunken brawl one night down in "The Flats", a rough neighborhood in Brownwood, Texas. Drugs and alcohol are not "cool and trendy". They are stupid and dangerous. They are demons which promise to help you deal with the raging sea but end up pulling you down to a watery grave.

One day, I was approached by Eric who had managed to scrounge up from someone a few hits of LSD type "acid" that he termed "Yellow Barrels". Yes, the kind that makes you see pink polka dotted elephants and flying bunny rabbits. Where he got them I could not tell, but Eric was resourceful like that... when we had no cow patties to tempt us.

Spiraling Towards Hell & Happily Deluded Along The Way!

It was a Friday night and we were hitting the local pinball, billiards and skate arena where we would hear REO Speedwagon blaring "I'm gonna keep on loving you" and check out the girls. We managed to drink beer at first to give us enough buzz to bravely slur our speech and act like fools in front of the girls we wanted so desperately to impress. As usual, we left the place without a single girl hanging on us. Except Eric who had Sandra, but he was still scoping out other "chicks" when she wasn't paying attention... or was she? Sandra ended up leaving us that night too. We went over to smoke pot with another stoner head who had a few joints to pass around at a nearby trailer park. It was there that Eric gave me the hits of acid. He gave me two and said it was okay because they were small and the high would be amazing. Up to this point I had never taken any drug harder than marijuana or gas fumes really. I don't know why I trusted my gas huffing, anything smoking, devil worshiping best friend, but I did.

After taking the hits, I had started having the most bizarre hallucinations. They just kept getting weirder and weirder. I became very disoriented and paranoid. I started hallucinating demonic imagery and felt like my soul was slipping into Hell itself. I felt my soul wanting to leave my body without the premeditated astral projection techniques. I thought I was really dying. I panicked. I wanted it to stop but it kept going. I was so scared. Someone at the party saw me glitching out and called Marvin, my step dad to come pick me up. I rode in his VW Bug all the way home, clinging to the backseat, petrified in fear. It was then that I made my very first sincere prayer to God. "God, if you can hear me, please take this high from me. Don't let me die and go to Hell. Please take these hallucinations from me. If you do, I promise I won't ever take acid again!"

I really felt like the devil was trying to kill me.... and you know something, he most assuredly was.

I got home and went to my room, where I finally fell asleep after counting pink elephants jumping over fences on my bedroom wall. I woke up the next morning and remembered my prayer. I actually thanked God and I kept my promise to Him. After this, I never took any drugs harder than marijuana.

The raging sea almost swallowed me up. But it was not my only brush with death.

For just a few months later, I would come literally inches away from certain death.

ECHO: DON'T FEAR THE REAPER

Tommy, Marvin's cousin, was an alcoholic with a capital B... B for Beer. I think that's why Tommy wanted to drive our newly acquired flatbed pickup into Brownwood. He wanted to buy a 12 pack since the only store in Blanket didn't sell any. Eric was out doing who knows what. I wanted to ride along to try to pick me up some cigarettes doing the "five finger discount", or in my case, the "three and a couple nubs discount". I was pretty proficient at stealing.

We started off from Blanket but the dynamic duo, Super Beer Drinker and I, his sidekick, Stoner Teen Without A Buzz forgot one major component when driving gas guzzling truck beasts. We forgot to get gas. So we promptly ran out of gas just as we hit the highway to Brownwood. Tommy pulled the truck over to the side of the highway and said he would go run and get a container of "petro-juice". He wanted me to wait for him in the truck. Tommy left promptly and I sat in the truck on a hot summer's day. The inside of the truck became unbearable, so I jumped out, found my way to the back and sat at the edge dangling my feet off of the flat bed. I must have sat there for about fifteen minutes wondering when Tommy was coming back, when all of a sudden I found myself being propelled ten feet in the air, then hitting a patch of grass, laying flat on my back. I looked behind me to see the back of the flat bed truck all smashed up, having also propelled forward by about twenty yards or so into a ditch. It hardly registered what had just taken place.

Apparently, a dude had just run his Datsun Pup truck into the back of the flatbed truck and his truck was totaled. I got up literally scared out of my gourd. I looked at the flatbed truck and where I had been sitting. It was all banged up! I wondered, "How did I just survive that?" I couldn't remember the truck heading towards me or the actual impact. Either God just sent an angel to propel me into the air before the crash somehow, or I was sitting only inches away from where the Datsun had struck and the brute force of impact did the propelling... either way, it was a total miracle I didn't have my legs immediately severed and the rest of my head and body thrown violently into the windshield of that truck! I was just spared from certain death! At that thought, I just freaked out and began running away from the reaper and the swipe of his sickle still swooshing nearby. I must have run about thirty seconds towards home when I heard a faint groan coming from the totaled Datsun. I stopped and wondered if I should turn back and help the guy. "How could he have survived?" The front of his truck was scrunched up like a flattened aluminum beer can. I turned back and started towards him. Before I even reached him, other cars had stopped and people were assisting the guy in the Datsun.

I couldn't believe it! The guy was pulled out of the driver's side without one freaking scratch on him! He had gotten banged up but no blood anywhere. Looking at his truck, and the flat bed, you could tell a miracle had just taken place. His truck only had a small pocket on the driver's side that hadn't crumpled from the force of impact. The pocket that saved his life. I remember the officer who came to the scene was in total amazement that both the Datsun driver and I had come out of the accident without a scratch. He said something like, "Someone is sure watching over you guys."

Although I was not impacted by the accident in any physical way other than tumbling down on my rumpus, the spiritual impact of that crash got my little heart beating faster and faster towards finding a sustainable answer as to why I was alive and even existed. And why had devils been hired out recently to try to assassinate me?

Oh no... another "Dad Rant" coming on!

At that time, I seriously contemplated on how our finite existence is so very fragile. We could be fit as a fiddle and choke to death on a vitamin tablet. We could tie our shoes in the morning in excitement for incredible plans for the new day, yet before the day is half over someone else is untying those same shoes in a morgue somewhere. Ninety nine point something percent of everyone who woke up this morning didn't schedule in their death today. I bet you didn't. We just have this lifelong habit of believing that death is for wrinkly old people or very unlucky, clumsy souls. Even when we become wrinkly old people, we assume death is not on the calendar between Bingo and our weekly enema. We never contemplate our mortal condition and how all of us are just a few skipped, frail heartbeats away from the dark unknown beyond the grave. Being that death is so sudden, uncertain, and sobering, you would think we would give more thought to the subject. The Bible says, *"Someone who is always thinking about his happiness is a fool. A wise person thinks about his death." Ecclesiastes 7:14*

Since death is such a permanent, indelible truth in this world, we should make it a priority to investigate it and any "considerable facts" within the scope of our very fragile existence. Many of us obsess about making sure we research thoroughly about a new house or car we're going to buy, reading reviews, manufacturing specs, etc. But how many of us think to thoroughly research out our soul in regards to death and what it may mean? Don't you think a possible conscious existence in some state of being for all eternity might be investigated religiously as an utmost priority? No pun intended. Yet the devils of indifference and ignorance just keep whispering in our souls, "You don't wanna know and you don't wanna care." Until a brush with death shocks us into the reality that we are fragile mortals.

I think Death 101 is a course we should all take until we have exhausted all the angles of truth on the subject. For many days after that swooshing brush with death on the back of that truck, I would look up from my pillow at the ceiling in my room, pondering my feeble life. I would wonder that had I died, what would have become of me. Would I just cease to exist? Would I truly go to an everlasting fire pit where I would burn for ever and ever and ever? Eternity in fiery Hell seemed like a sadistic punishment for my petty, insignificant life of sin, but what did I know? My real father had been sadistic at times, so perhaps God was too? Would I just float about as a wandering ghost on the earth, haunting houses and scaring families with small children? What was the afterlife and did I really have a soul? Maybe the atheists are right and my consciousness is just a sadistic joke of random chance and evolution. Maybe if I had died, I would have faded to black, lost consciousness and become just "dust in the wind". That seemed just as scary to me as eternal burning in Hell. Like all of us, I wanted to live... and live forever... but not like this, in a harsh and unforgiving raging sea of abuse, worthlessness, purposelessness, uncertainty and fear.

I needed answers about the raging sea within me and the raging sea around me. However, I would have to wait a few more months before a "great reveal" would change my life forever.

ECHO: RAGING SEA, BE STILL!

Sometime in the autumn of 1982, my Grandpa and Grandma Goodman called us. They talked with Seany and I about the possibility of them coming through Texas to pick us up and take us with them to California. They were going to visit my father, Josie, and our two other brothers, John and Peter for Christmas. At first we sort of hem-hawed about going but ended up confirming we would go with them. Our father had not seen us since we had left him, running from his car in Indiana a few years previously.

Daddy had recently had his lower leg amputated from complications due to his Diabetes. I was also much older and more resourceful, so I didn't fear if Daddy tried to keep us there in California, where they had moved to. I surmised that Seany and I could easily outrun him and hitchhike our way back to Texas. But our Grandparents also told us that they would bring us back to Texas afterwards and we trusted them.

As a matter of fact, Grandpa and Grandma Goodman were the only anchors in my raging sea, besides my Mama who wasn't really an anchor...she was more like a slow leaking rubber raft I hung onto for dear life. But Grandpa and Grandma were the only people I respected as "real Christians". So when the day came for them to pick us up for the Christmas visit, both Seany and I cut our hair from hippy length to a nice "Buster Brown" look. I didn't want to cut my long, flowing blonde locks but Mama thought it best. I also didn't want to "frighten the children" of any of the Goodman clan in California.

We were apprehensive about seeing our father but we were also somewhat excited about visiting California, the land of Cheech and Chong. So I left Eric in Texas to be the custodian of my room and my vinyl rock and roll record collection while I was away.

When Grandpa and Grandma came, I decided to

temporarily quit smoking cigarettes while visiting California. I had been smoking one pack a day. It was hard to go cold turkey but I knew I would not be able to smoke anytime that week. I would have to leave my cigarettes with Eric too.

During that holiday visit, I saw a completely changed father. He was definitely not the same Daddy we grew up with. I am sure he wasn't perfect and still had bouts with the raging sea within him, but during that visit, I never saw my father get angry even one time. He never raised his voice or shouted. He never said an unkind word to us or to his other sons John and Peter.

As a matter of fact, he was way more gentle, patient and kind than I remembered. He was more the Dad that we saw little glimpses of when we were growing up, when he did treat us well. But there was something else about him and his home that was very different. I felt an unseen presence. I felt a warmth like the warmth of a fireplace flickering flames on a cold winter night.

That week our Dad took us all around sight seeing in California. We went panning for gold at a creek nearby known for finding gold nuggets. He took us to his church. We also went to SeaWorld with Grandpa and Grandma but because of my father's amputated foot, he could not go with us. Instead, our father went to visit prisoners at a local prison where he led a Bible study that he called "SEEK". I remember the title because it reverberated in my own spirit at the time. What were these men seeking after and why?

Although my father had become a real Christian, he didn't push Jesus down my throat that Christmas week. He just let his light so shine. I remember I woke up early one morning at his home. I accidentally opened the door to his bedroom where I saw him kneeling, deep in prayer. It made a lasting impression on me. "Why was Daddy praying so intensely and so early in the morning? He seemed like he really believed that God was up there listening to him. Was God the presence that I felt?

After the week long visit had come to an end, my father prayed with us and gave Seany and I one of his signature "bear hugs". It had been a nice visit getting to see "John John" and Peter whom we had never really gotten to know. Josie was so very pleasant as well. She seemed much happier than we'd ever known.

Departing from Daddy's home after the week was up was not as easy as I imagined. I thought I would actually get bored and want to run back to Texas to resume my thug life. I actually found myself yearning to stay longer.

It was January 1st 1983. Grandpa and Grandma were driving us back to Texas through California, Arizona and to the border of Texas when a snowstorm hit. It wasn't a life threatening severe one, but it kept Grandpa driving a lot longer, sometimes completely stopped on the highway. Both Grandpa and Grandma were people of few words, not chatty at all. They were not preachy or trying to persuade us to believe. Just people who let there light so shine.

So returning to Texas we had miles and miles of dead silence and time to reflect. Both Seany and I had exhausted all ways to keep us occupied or entertained. We just sat in the backseat staring out the window into the snowy landscape.

I found myself reflecting a whole lot. Thank God, Iphones had not been invented yet to keep us distracted from thinking deeper than silly Facebook posts or bedazzling app games. Entertainment keeps us mostly from meditating on the issues of the heart, personal reflection and deep self examination. The devil likes this age of gadgets and gizmos which keep men's souls entertained all the way to Hell.

There was a gnawing heartache inside of me as we slowly rode along, that opened up into a grand canyon of emptiness and loneliness. I couldn't believe it! I was actually yearning to go back to California to be with my father! I sat there wondering what it was that I was missing so much. What was it about my time in California that tore at my soul to return? I kept thinking about these things and then it hit me. In the whole time I was there, I felt peace. I felt the resolute peace that my Grandpa and

Grandma had and that my father now had. The raging sea had ceased to exist in those seemingly happy moments with Daddy, Josie, John and Peter. I wasn't so naive to believe that a perfect world had entered into Daddy's home but I knew a peaceful one had settled there... at least one that the sea was not so raging anymore.

I had left my father's home that so vastly contrasted the place I was now returning to... Drunken fights, fear of death and destruction, hangovers and endless partying, celebrating always with a beer and a buzz... and for what? I had no clue. I had no real life there. No purpose, no worthy causes, just self centeredness and a dog eat dog world of lying, thieving, sex, drugs and Rock N Roll. I sat there realizing my whole life in Texas was just an endless loop of trying to desperately fulfill physical pleasures and entertainments with no admirable life goals or ambitions. I reflected on my heart of bitterness and darkness... how I was unforgiving, unmerciful, vindictive, hateful, murderous and how that whole scene of the hippie lifestyle was really not that "cool" after all. I was returning to this raging sea that I had for a moment in California forgotten all about.

Grandpa was driving in the whiteout of snow, but all I could see ahead of us was a road going nowhere. I found myself yearning for a new life, a different life, a life where I could be free from this feeling that I was always drowning, always one or two thrashes away from giving up to a watery grave. Inside I was crying out for freedom. Deep down, we all want this freedom.

We then got stuck in a snow-laden, traffic stand still on I20. As we sat there, unable to move, something inwardly pushed forward. In a flash of a moment in the backseat of my Grandparent's car, my inward tears fell upward. I found myself praying sincerely to a God I did not know, to a Savior I did not trust or believe in.

"God, if you're up there, I want you to change my life. I want a new life. I want to be different. I don't like who I am or how I'm living. Please, if you're up there, change my life." I prayed this

99

simple prayer without any other motives or agendas. It was not eloquent or "highly spiritual". It was just heartfelt and broken. No pride, no ego, no justifying myself or my sins. This is exactly what God looks for in repentant souls... God grants miracles to the broken and humble. *"He heals the brokenhearted and binds up their wounds." Psalms 147:3*

It was an incredible moment as soon as the last syllable left my thoughts in that prayer. Poof, almost instantly I felt this weight of a burden of guilt, shame and festering emptiness just completely disappear in my heart. I actually felt a joy unspeakable rise up within me at that moment. I turned to my brother who was on the other side of the backseat staring out the window. He looked deep in thought himself.

My habit of self doubting kicked in and I wondered if what I was experiencing was really from God. I prayed, "God if this is real..." and then randomly thought, "If this is really from you and you heard my prayer, let my brother Seany start to sing." I don't know why I prayed that. Seany never normally burst out in song because he wasn't much of a singer. All of a sudden, Seany blurts out from the silence in a whispered singsong, "Jesus loves me this I know for the Bible tells me so!" Seany then says "Let's all sing!" Grandpa quickly responded, "Sure Sean, let's sing." Sean started singing softly again in the backseat behind grandma. "Jesus loves me this I know for the Bible tells me so!" Unbeknownst to me, my brother Seany was also being touched by God.

At that moment when Seany began to sing, my heart just turned into an organ of musical notes and I chimed in too. It was an amazing feeling! The God of the universe had just stopped what He was doing in Heaven and looked down on Earth, in a snowstorm on a frozen highway in Texas, to a little slow moving sedan, to a little 15 year old raggedy heart like mine and heard my prayer! My soul had been touched by the Creator of the world and He had commanded in that very moment to my soul, "Raging sea, be still!"

ECHO: STUMBLING BLOCKS REMOVED

After we finally made it back to Texas and Grandpa and Grandma said goodbye, I left them feeling happy for God's touch on my soul, yet sad to see those two precious, beautiful anchors drive away. I didn't share with them what I had prayed or how God confirmed to me His love. I just kept pondering this new "God perspective" in my heart. As Seany and I grabbed our luggage to bring to our room to unpack, I suddenly felt like a "stranger in a strange land". How was I to live as a new creation in this old drug and alcohol culture that surrounded me?

No one other than Seany had really tried to live a Christian life in this environment. Seany had gotten touched by God a year or so earlier at a little Baptist church and had come home claiming to be a "Christian".

At that time, everyone in the family except Mama laughed at him and taunted him for his new found faith. Unfortunately, I was one of them who mocked him. Seany, being around 11 at the time, seemed to change for a good while, but having no real guidance or support from his family, he slipped back into his old life. When God touched him on the California trip, he reaffirmed his faith and we had briefly compared notes. Both of us were going to try to brave the raging sea, with God at the helm of our ship.

Eric, my best friend suddenly appeared out of nowhere, wearing a bandana to keep his long hair from making him look like an Old English Sheepdog. He looked at both Seany and I and smiled real big. "Hey man, you're back! Let's celebrate and go get stoned out of our gourds!"

I just stood there in a daze. Eric looked different to me. He looked, at that moment, not as my best friend but as an unfamiliar soul. Even worse... an enemy. How could I live for God and be different in this same environment? Jesus had spoken to the raging sea in me to "Be still", but the raging sea around me continued as usual. I was trying to compose my thoughts and words to tell him that I gave my life to Jesus, but Seany beat me to it. He looked at Eric in the eyeballs and said, "Eric, we've become Christians!" Now when Seany said that, you could have inserted a special echo effect in that moment, "Eric, we've become Christians... Christians... Christians..." because Eric had an over the top reaction that I still to this day have not fully figured out. Eric looked at me for confirmation and I just nodded my head in agreement, not saying a word. All at once, Eric's eyes bulged out and he screamed out a raging sea of a roar, "Ahhhhhhhhhhhh!!!" He took off running to my room where he hurriedly stuffed his duffle bag with what little clothes and stuff that he had. He never looked me in the eye, nor did I try to stop him from leaving. I just stood there observing his crazed reaction.

Eric put his duffle bag around his shoulder and took off down the road, not even saying "Goodbye", his tromping figure slowly disappearing in the distance. I never once spoke to or saw Eric again, ever... in my entire life! He just suddenly vanished from the raging sea.

Looking back at it, I realize now what happened and why he furiously exited the scene of my life. If God hadn't taken away Eric, I might not be here sharing with you now. I don't know. Eric would have surely tried to chip away at my resolve to live for Jesus. I might have fallen back into my old life and shipwrecked my faith.

To this day, I pray for Eric, that wherever he is, God would touch his life like He did mine. The last I heard about him through the grapevine, Eric had been caught by the police trying to smuggle M16's across the Canadian border. For whatever reason, God forced my best friend, who had a major influence over my psyche, to completely vanish out of my life. God helps us dodge bullets we can't even see at the time they are fired at us.

Especially as a new born Christian, God sometimes will remove people from our lives who otherwise would be a major stumbling block to our growth.

Yes, God believes in the freedom of disassociation. It's not bad, "racist" or evil to cut off people from our lives who could potentially destroy our faith or walk with God. Jesus said, "*If any man come to me, and hate not his father, and mother, and wife, and children, and brothers, and sisters, yes, and his own life also, he cannot be my disciple.*" *Luke 14:26* This word is translated "hate" but actually just means "to love less than". What Jesus was saying, using hyperbole and metaphors in most of his teachings is that God wants you to love and follow after Him with so much commitment and intensity that it may seem like at times that you don't love or care for anyone else in your life. We are commanded to love others. This is a truth undisputed, but we are to love God our Creator and Savior above all others. So at times, we must choose God's path above those we love who may want us to go down a different one. In the end, when we choose to love God supremely, who is Love, then we love others properly... directly and indirectly.

ECHO: NOT OUT OF THE WOODS YET

Several weeks had passed since my soul had been touched by God.

Back in 9th grade, where I had made straight F's and had planned to quit school that year altogether, I started applying myself in the new year with a new heart. I actually got my first B on a test since elementary school. I was maintaining faith but I was struggling with the elements around me. A smoke filled home made it hard. I was struggling to keep from going back to smoking cigarettes. I was tempted to get high and drink alcohol. I was fighting with these strong urges in my flesh that had become addictions.

When I was away from them completely in California, it was much easier, but being in the midst of the melting pot of this culture in Texas made it almost impossible. I thought maybe I should call my father and tell him I had become a Christian, and even discuss living with him. But the love for Mama prevailed and I could not leave her heartbroken. I would stay in the lion's den where I was not sure I would survive.

I pressed on fighting the strong temptations. I was dangling off the edge of my faith, ready at any moment to plunge back into that raging sea, which I had told God I never wanted to go back to. My spirit man was so changed, so ready to conquer the raging sea but I realized my flesh was still so very strong. The raging sea within me had not magically disappeared altogether. I still had fits of anger. I still had temptations to lust, to lie, to steal, to be manipulative. I still craved cigarettes and the ability to take something to numb my brain from pain.

Everyone around me was still happily deranged and drowning, thrashing in the raging sea. I wanted to completely disembark from the drug culture, but didn't know how to do that in the environment I was trapped in.

I was so close to giving up when suddenly I got a phone

call from my Grandpa Goodman. His voice was cracking and grieved.

"Heath, your father has had a major heart attack. We thought he was gone but they revived him and he's hanging in there."

My heart sank. I had wanted to tell my father about my coming to faith and his witness that helped me. "Is he going to make it Grandpa?"

"He's not out of the woods yet. Pray for him Heath."

"Okay yes, I will pray for him." I could tell Grandpa was really worried. I hung up the phone with my head spinning and my heart churning. I told Seany and Mama.

I knew I had to pray. I ran into the bathroom and locked the door. I got on my knees by the bathtub. My heart was wrenching. My tears fell upwards.

"God, I know you've seen my struggle lately with wanting to smoke cigarettes and my other temptations. I am trying to live for you but it's so hard! Forgive me for failing and for wanting to give up. I don't want to go back to that life. But God, I really need you to be with my Daddy right now. I forgive him for all those years he abused me. He was struggling with lots of pain then and now he's serving you. Heal him God, don't let him die! I want to be able to tell him in person that I forgive him and that I love him. I want to tell him that his changed life helped to change mine. I want to be able to receive one of his bear hugs!"

I cried and prayed hard. "Jesus, if you heal my Daddy, I promise I won't ever look back. I will serve you and I won't pick up cigarettes or go back to drinking or doing drugs. Just please heal my Daddy, please!!!"

I ended my prayer believing God was going to heal my father.

It was late that same evening when the phone rang again. It was Grandpa. I hoped he had good news for me but why call at this time of night? His voice was shaky and sad. My heart sank.

"Heath, your father has passed away. He's gone home to be

105

with Jesus."

I froze in my emotions. "What?"

"Yes, Heath, your father had complications. He was coherent for a little while. I told him we were praying for him and he signaled with his hands that he was praying too. But after a little while longer his heart just gave out."

No sooner than I got off the phone with Grandpa, my whole body began to shake uncontrollably. Seany had been up playing video games when Mama told him. We both cried. I was shaking so much that I laid with my Mama all night in her bed. I had lost my father. He was gone. I would never see him again in this life. I knew I had forgiven him but I didn't get the chance to tell him. I wanted so bad to share with him how God had touched my heart. I wanted to have the father and son relationship that we never had.

I really wanted to take one of those snapshots of a happy childhood moment with Daddy on his sailboat or when we went camping. I wanted to make it into a feature film now that both of our lives had been changed by God. We could start anew, father and son.

But God took him and there was nothing I could do. I would only see him again in the new Heavens and new Earth, in the age to come.

I was disappointed that God had not answered my prayer to heal my father, but I knew God's answers are not always what we want or think is right. After I saw Daddy lying in the casket at his funeral, knowing he was no longer suffering, I prayed this in my heart.

"God, I know my Daddy is with you. I know I will get a chance to see him again and we will have the conversation that we never got to have down here. I know I promised you that I would really serve you and not look back if you healed my Daddy... and even though it wasn't the way I wanted, you did heal my Daddy... completely and forever. He has no more pain, no more suffering from severe diabetes, no more amputated foot or all the other things he suffered from in this world. Since you answered my prayer to an even greater degree, I am going to keep my promise to you. I love you God... and give a bear hug to my Daddy just for me."

The raging sea doesn't want us to call upon God or trust Him, even when things don't make sense. As finite beings, we somehow think that if we can pray a certain prayer and sound sincere enough to God, our maker, that we can manipulate Him to do what we want Him to do... to answer our prayers the way we envision them to be answered. But God transcends the raging sea and all the souls thrashing about in it. He knows the greater story unfolding. He sees where we cannot.

It is easy for us to get mad at God and blindly raise a fist in the air to blame Him, raging against heaven for the raging sea around us. It's easy to rebel against Him, and justify why we won't serve a God whom we perceive has done us wrong or allowed us to suffer in the raging sea. It is hard to go against our flesh and our own reasoning to instead stand with God even when we do not understand His ways. But like a small boy who wants to play in the middle of a busy road, not comprehending the violence of cars crashing into him, he finally submits to his loving father's instruction, not because he fully understands why he must obey or submit, but just because he has simply learned to trust his Daddy. Because he knows he loves him. We, as finite creatures with a limited understanding of the raging sea, must never blame God for it but trust Him that He has a plan, a purpose for us in it and to eventually transcend it.

After my father's heart attack, my Grandpa said, "He wasn't out of the woods yet". I know this was his way of coping and hoping that his son would recover. But little did Grandpa realize that "the woods" meant the raging sea my father lived and thrashed about in all his life. When Jesus took him, my father truly was now "out of the woods". I can also say that my father's death, to some degree of metaphor, took me "out of the woods". This is because I had not so resolutely committed my life to God until Daddy's death reminded me of the frailness and futility of life in the raging sea. I realized that if I was to ever transcend the raging sea in me and around me, I must do it with Jesus at my helm. I must do it His way and not lean on my finite understanding and my fickle heart.

ECHO: BEFORE & AFTER PICS

Before Jesus:
Notice The Sad, Troubled Eyes

After Jesus: Notice The Happy,
Peaceful Eyes (Not The Baby's!)

My testimony really has little to do with what I was before Christ began rescuing me in the raging sea. I say "in the raging sea" because neither you nor I can be completely free from the raging sea as long as we are alive in this fallen world. Some of you can relate to my story and some of you probably think to yourself, "Man, Heath thinks he had it rough... just listen to my raging sea stories!" It's the ol' "my battle scar is bigger than yours" thingy. Well, I am sure you have victim stories to tell or maybe some you'd rather not. I too have other stories in my raging sea that I could share, but I dare not because I don't think it's expedient or relevant to open up every skeleton in the family closet. Let's just suffice it to say, we all are wicked and victimized people to the core without God... just like the rest of all humanity.

Now, if we've never had a revelation of our own wickedness, then I doubt we've had a real revelation of the Savior's atoning sacrifice or a real saving knowledge of the gospel. The gospel is for sinners. So if you've never been one, how can you be saved from something you don't need saving from?

We are all sinners without God. It's just that some of us get deceived about what constitutes sin. We try to justify ourselves before God and others. ***"The heart is deceitful above all things***

and desperately wicked, who can know it?" *Jeremiah 17:9* This is why we should refrain from sitting on a self righteous high horse trying to judge the hearts of others. We can't even discern how wicked our own hearts are without the Holy Spirit, so how can we rightly judge others?

But I must make myself clear in an age of ludicrous tolerance and lawlessness- We can't judge the hearts of others, but we can judge others to some degree based on their outward actions and obvious visual aspects. In a world where ""Don't judge me" has become synonymous with "Let's all just endorse and tolerate what clearly is a moral failure." Yes, we can't be God and judge the hearts of individuals based on no evidence or even scanty, unreliable or unsubstantiated circumstances and hearsay.

But we can make judgments based on observable and obvious facts and data. A thief that is caught red-handed stealing something from a store might say "Don't judge me, I accidentally stuck the item under my pants and shirt and walked out forgetting to pay for it!" But his actions, his darting eyes and suspicious behavior are a huge indicator of guilt. As we could also say for clear and obvious facts for murderers, liars and sexually perverse people, such as pedophiles and sodomites. We can't walk around like zombies, never making obvious judgment calls because we dare not call sin sin or distinguish between right and wrong.

Yet in this day of "I'm okay, you're okay- everything's permissible as long as you identify with it as part of who you are" kind of delusional culture that we compromise to fit in. Like in the parable of the Emperor's New Clothes, no one is supposed to tell the king that he's naked. No one dares express the moral absolutes set and bound in the Holy Scriptures lest sinners get offended. We are supposed to go along with the delusional madness, because it's hip and trendy to never take a stand or draw a logical or moral line in the sand.

So I have been transparent with you on some of my childhood experiences for a specific reason. I am ashamed of my past and do not justify one bit of the sin and debauchery.

I shared it, not so religious people can sit on a high horse of moral superiority and judge me, my father, my mother or my other family members in light of our godless and troubled past. I shared it for the down to earth sinners and ragamuffins who might find hope in relating to what I have gone through... to be encouraged that if I can be rescued from the raging sea in me and around me (not that I have been totally rescued yet), so can anyone... so can you!

Our real testimony begins when we become believers, and the living, resurrected Christ begins to break us and make us into the person He envisions us to be.

However, I will say this, the mark of true conversion is a changed life. *"Therefore if any man be in Christ, he is a new creature: old things are passed away; behold, all things are become new." 2 Corinthians 5:17* If we are never changed, what are we converted from? Today, a lot of people claim to be Christian but still remain happy in their sin and bitter hearts. When we are truly converted, we then begin a journey of sanctification and transformation.

You see, conversion or even what we call "being born again" is not an event that happens to us one moment in time but is more a continual process of birth, growth and maturity. I am still being converted... still changing... still being born again in new things.... still being transformed. This is the common experience with all those who truly become Christians. Salvation is a lifelong transformation and covenant with God. We are all on a journey. Some of us travel faster and develop quickly more defined principles and truth. Others of us, for whatever reason, take a lot of hard knocks until the fog of our self centered lives is lifted and we start seeing victory over the flesh, the devil and sin. We must love one another on this journey and be patient with one another in the process. Knowing and obeying the Word of God does help speed up the process.

I was baptized at age 15 at the Blanket First Baptist Church in the spring of 1983. This was the first church I attended as a new believer. In 1983 it seemed to be very much a stereotypical little Southern Baptist church, mostly comprised of sweet little old ladies and stoic old men being dragged along beside them. There were hardly any young couples, teens or even small children. I felt a little out of place. My Mama and Sean would attend with me sometimes. We would sing old time gospel hymns in ritual fashion, then listen to drab announcements, dry prayers and a 30 minute sleepy sermonette. Not trying to be mean, but as Vance Havner wrote, we generally "started the service at 11 o'clock sharp and would leave at 12 noon dull". The minister was a cordial and humble man but he was not what you would call a dynamic or inspirational preacher. The sermons were sort of low key, country fried messages smothered in a little scriptural gravy. I only attended for about a year until a friend and coworker invited me to attend his church in Brownwood.

I began to attend Milton Avenue Baptist Church. It was totally different than my experience at Blanket First Baptist. It was Bapticostal if there is such a creature. For one, they had a lot of young couples, teens and children. This is the same church My brother Sean had professed Christ when he was 11. The worship was contemporary and very spiritually oriented. It was inspiring and I felt the presence of God in worship. Then I heard the minister preach. Pastor JV preached with fervor. He preached with fire in his eyes. It was a far cry from the monotonous messages of my previous pastor. I hadn't realized that the gospel actually could make men so excited and passionate. I enjoyed his messages very much. Even the ones that brought me under conviction of Holy Spirit. We had altar calls every week and I was usually up there repenting of something or just wanting to get closer to God. Pastor JV was a "Revival Preacher" and would also go to churches and preach "Revivals".

Soon enough, Pastor JV took me and a group of other young men under his mentorship. Pastor JV and the elders "licensed" me to preach the gospel in 1985. I was 18 years old. I put licensed in quotes because I now believe that God licenses every believer to preach the gospel. I guess the only difference is that the piece of paper gave me a license to marry or bury people by the State as well. Pastor JV began introducing me to what he called the great men of God and Revivalists of the past.

As a new believer, I went from milk to meat in a short period of time. Pastor JV gave me authors like Vance Havner, A.W. Tozer, Charles Spurgeon, John Wesley and Charles Finney. I devoured the books and my spiritual knowledge and hunger increased quickly. However, in hindsight, I think being introduced to these

Preacher Boy With My Nephew Mickey

very deep and spiritually disciplined men of God did me a little disservice.

You see, spiritual knowledge is all well and good. but unless it is coupled with a true and deepening relationship with God, it can lead to what I would call "religious pride" and "spiritual elitism". The Apostle Paul says "knowledge puffs up".

Unfortunately, I went from feeling blessed to read those books to being privileged to "higher knowledge" than the common ordinary yokels. Nonetheless, I began developing undercurrents of some religious pride and haughty thoughts of superiority in my walk with God. Not to his discredit, but Pastor JV made us young men feel special and "called to greatness". So when I began to preach, I had a little of this pride and religiosity in me. I started turning down a pathetic, religious egocentric path.

Yes, here comes a Dad rant.

It's important to encourage and mentor young men and women to be all they can be for Christ, but to temper "spiritual knowledge" as rather a pursuit of knowing God personally. it's more than just reading books about Him and gaining an academic grasp of truth. Men who have neither Bible or Christian books have come out of prison or dire circumstances as "spiritual giants" because they simply pursued knowing God in prayer. Books, even the Bible, can be a dead letter, a dry intellectual piece of knowledge in our minds rather than an authentic knowing of Christ intimately in our hearts and spirits. Christ is a real and living person who we all can come to know genuinely.

The devil is into counterfeiting a "knowledge about God" rather than knowing God personally and intimately. He will sabotage your pure devotion to a living Messiah and God to replace it with a placebo religious experience. GK Chesterton once quipped, *"Let your religion be less of a theory and more of a love affair."* Many of us live as if Christ is a theoretical concept rather than a living, lovely personable entity. Just because much of Christianity is filled with plastic people who are pretending to serve God by way of ritual and religiosity doesn't mean you or I have to do the same.

The main reason we sometimes circumvent or short circuit a real relationship with God is because the Holy Spirit, in my experience, is an ever present comforter and convictor of the heart (yes, we like comfort but not so much conviction- contrary to popular culture, shame and guilt are actually good things to push us towards change).

As a teacher, Holy Spirit is always working on our true inward character. This can be a tough and heart wrenching process toward our sanctification and acceptance of truth. We would rather bypass the Holy Spirit's crucial work in our hearts and settle for either ritual, dead religion or hyper-spiritual experiences that constantly entertain or excite our flesh. It's the extreme opposites in Christendom- on one hand, a total orthodoxy and robotic ritualism or on the other hand, a weird, way out and sometimes downright wacky super-spiritualism.

I've been there and done that with all those things. But I can tell you now with 100% certainty, a real and personal relationship with Jesus is a road less traveled, but is way more fulfilling (and actually a pleasant and easier road), than falling into dead churchianity, silly hyper-spiritualism or backsliding into sinfulness.

Anyways, I continued to be a part of Milton Ave Baptist Church for about three years. However, due to God's loving dedication to my ultimate character development, I changed churches in 1986. I began attending a little church called Church Of The Lord Jesus. It was a nondenominational "holiness church". Here is where much of my spiritual roots would be planted and grow. Pastor Green was and still is as far as I know, a real man of God and man of prayer. He continues, to this day, to be a friend in my life. He and his wife have an incredible, almost unbelievable, powerful testimony of tragedy and triumph.

Pastor Green was also a passionate preacher. What struck me when I first heard and met him was that he was authentic and real in his love for God. He would weep and plead from the pulpit as if he really believed souls were lost, dying and heading for destruction. His preaching was truly heartfelt and had a profound effect on me.

Pastor Green was (and still is) a humble man with an incredible background. He and his wife lost their little boy to a horrendous murder and almost lost their toddler daughter as well. But God performed a verifiable miracle in the hospital and their daughter was instantly healed from life threatening injuries. When I first heard his testimony, I thought to myself, "This man has suffered tremendously and instead of bitterly walking away from God, he drew passionately closer to Him." The more I heard Pastor Green preach, the more I wanted to walk with God like him. He became a sort of hero of the faith to me. Don't get me wrong, he was not a perfect man or preacher, but I sensed he was a genuine man of God in a world full of phonies.

At any rate, I spent over a decade in the church and my faith and knowledge grew exponentially there. Yes, there were lots of ups and downs going to the Church of the Lord Jesus. There were things done and said that were not always consistent with the God I was coming to know. We got caught up in a bit of legalism and religiosity too. There were church splits and the church dwindled down to just a few families.

I had a habit of putting men of God on pedestals and Pastor Green was no exception. God finally got through to me one day as I heard Him clearly say to me, "Heath, you must follow Me, not men, not even your own heart. They will all fail you! You yourself will fail you! Put your faith in no one but me." Don't get me wrong, I still to this day esteem real men of God with high respect, but I also know they are fallible, fallen and need Jesus just as much as the next ragamuffin. Even the most honorable, God fearing man or woman can fail, can falter, can even completely fall away. The Apostle Paul said he could. It's so important never to allow your own disappointments and disillusionments in mere men or women to whisper a justification in your heart for why you can no longer serve God.

On that final day, we can't tell God that we turned away or rebelled because of so and so. We are accountable for our own lives. Jesus demonstrated a true sacrificial love for us. No one should earn your respect and worship more than the One who died for you. Admire Him alone; no other deserves first place. He will never fail you!

Also, a quick note about holiness and "holiness people". Just as I have a true burden for people caught up in sin, I also have a true burden for people caught up in "holiness" or what they might assume is true holiness. Being that I had experienced a "holiness church" in the late eighties and nineties, I used to think that holiness was all about women wearing long dresses, long hair and long faces.

Of course, I think many of us genuinely loved God back then, but we fell into the trap of religiosity and the "pride of religion". John Wesley once wrote, *"If the devil can't get you to take pleasure in your sin, he'll get you to take pride in your virtue."* It's so true. If Satan can't trip us up with sin, he'll cultivate self righteousness and religious pride in us. Either way he has us and we are no longer effective or vibrant witnesses of God's grace and mercy. I came to see holiness as a strict religious discipline of do's and don'ts, a performance based churchianity. I became legalistic and judgmental. I became a Pharisee, and it was sad you see. (Some of you will get that.)

If our "holiness" distances ourselves or sets ourselves apart, where we are not accessible for every day sinners to be touched by the grace or the mercy of God from our own lives, then we do not have true holiness.

If our "holiness" is a joyless expression of do's and don'ts and we are only preaching judgement and "God's strict commandments and laws" then we do not understand what true holiness is and from whence it springs.

Am I saying we never preach about judgment, expose sin or or teach on God's commandments? No, not at all. But it is God's love, grace and mercy that must motivate sinners, not His wrath or law, which are still valid elements. *"It is the goodness of God that leads men to true repentance"*, not fire and brimstone or a scary message on Hell. If your Christian faith is only propelled by fear of Hell, then it will be found lacking and will falter in this wicked age. Christian faith must be propelled by genuine experience of knowing God, His love, mercy and grace.

If all we are is one big faultfinding, critical, strict religionist that can never crack a smile or stand in the presence of sinners sinning, then we're no use to the humble Savior who leaves the ninety-nine to find the one lost little lamb... or descends to the lowest pit of Hell to rescue the broken, dying, desperately decadent ones. Can your "holiness" embrace a smelly, cursing, drunken bum with God's love?

True "holiness" power is a man or woman of God who can live all around the sin and darkness but never be tempted by them. His "holiness" is no virtue of his own but only God within him (from the Holy Spirit), pushing out light and love, making a difference in this fallen, broken, mixed up world. Vance Havner once quipped, *"No one ever became holier by living in a hole and some of the greatest so called 'Christian Mystics' were mistakes."*

I do still believe that Christians need to live holy and separate from worldly and sinful temptations, but the secret to this is more easily accomplished by the Holy Spirit. He creates the character and nature of Christ in those who genuinely want to live holy and pleasing to God. Yet a heart still unregenerate, coveting after the refuse and sin-slime of the world, will put on "religion" and pretense as they try to be good enough to earn a spot in Heaven.

The truth is, *"This is the covenant I will make with them after that time, says the Lord. I will put my laws in their hearts, and I will write them on their minds." Hebrew 10:16*

The man steeped in religion says, "I'VE GOT to keep God's commandments. I'VE GOT to live holy!" The man who truly loves God and His ways, says "I GET to keep God's commandments. I GET to live holy!"

For the one steeped in religion, serving God and obedience to Him is a drudgery and a burdensome task, but to the one who has been authentically transformed by God's love, obedience and service, it's a wonderful privilege and gift he has been given.

So anyways, after over a decade of being at this holiness church, I felt God's nudging to move to East Texas and become part of YWAM (Youth With A Mission and Keith Green's Last Days Ministries). I loved Keith Green's music and the spirit of God that anoints his music to this day. I learned to play the piano myself with the few fingers I have and started writing music. Keith Green was a great inspiration to me. I would sing in churches and play the songs I wrote. God genuinely touched others through some of them. I had this vision that perhaps God would use me like Keith Green, and what better way to launch my "great and awesome" anointed ministry out of the same ministry as Keith Green.

However, God had other plans for me.

You see, it's easy to get ahead of God and think grandiose thoughts of being the next Keith Green or Billy Graham. But God's not interested in raising up anyone who has still got a lot of ego and self admiration. We might see visions of greatness to perfect our ministry, while God sees visions of grueling hardship to perfect our character. He took the great Moses, raised in royalty, to the backside of a desert for forty years in order to get him to the place of brokenness and meekness. God took Joseph through pits and prisons to humble him before he ever saw his dreams come true. King David had to live in rocks and caves fearing for his life before he ever sat on the throne, which was prophesied over him!

I went through YWAM and heard some very powerful challenges to the religiosity I had built up within myself. I started to actually see that I had become somewhat of a Pharisee. Oh, I genuinely loved God, but I allowed the devil to make me a proud, self reliant religionist to some degree. God began breaking this spirit within me at YWAM and Last Days Ministry.

For the first year or so at YWAM, I had saved up money to sustain me but it was dwindling fast. I finally got a few people to sponsor me as a "missionary in training" but the donations were meager. I lived on corn dogs, fish sticks and Ramen Noodles.

During this time I met some ragamuffin Christians in the making (like myself). I was genuinely humbled and the Lord had a real mess on His hands with me. Thank God for His steadfast love and patience. It took a lot to untangle my heart from a lot of religion and the sins that go with spiritual pride. I am pretty sure I am completely untangled now... aahh well, until God goes deeper, right? Truth is, I am still a work in progress.

ECHO: THIS IS FOR ALL THE LONELY PEOPLE

In YWAM, I did come out of some of my awkwardness around girls. I met a lot of girls who loved God and almost everyone of them I probably prayed, "Lord, is she the one?" You see, I also had a great desire to get married and had visions of sons and daughters running around my feet. Unfortunately, I was so unready in my character for such a relationship. I was half-baked, still doughy in the middle. I, like all of us, had a propensity to always make everything about me.

Self centeredness is the hallmark of individuality and human existence, right? Being around all these eligible sisters in the Lord at YWAM, I just assumed that God was soon going to direct me to "The One." I didn't even think that perhaps He was still busy untangling me from my spiritual ego and the screwed up insecurities from my childhood and "finger freak" identity. I was a ragamuffin mess, even in missionary school.

Because of being around all these beautiful, eligible Christian women in YWAM, I started focussing my mind and heart on finding "The One". I became very lonely as I played whack-a-mole with girl relationships that I was trying to cultivate into something more than friendship. I truly messed up my heart as I cultivated the wrong ones. A few times I got into serious relationships with girls that I knew deep down were not "The One". I broke some girls hearts as well as my own a million and one times. I was playing pinball with my heart as I jumped from trying to juggle girl friendships, purity of heart and slaying the beasts of insecurity and loneliness in my soul.

Much of our loneliness is a result of selfishness. (You can look inward now.) No one likes to be around needy, self-absorbed people. To have friends, we must be friendly and thinking of others rather than ourselves all the time.

If we are needy and leech onto others to drain them of their life force and resources, we will become more lonely and "needy" in the end. No one wants to be or stay in a lopsided relationship of all give and no take. Self-absorbed people are the most lonely, unfulfilled people in the world.

I was lonely. The Lord had become my second passion. My first passion was finding the girl of my dreams. Oh, I wanted her to be this glorious, Jesus loving woman of God, but I desired this more than the pursuit of Jesus. Each one of us are multifaceted people with a smorgasbord of motives, desires and agendas. Each one of us can truly have good motives and we can also have bad motives mixed in along the way. This is the fall of man and the "knowledge of good and evil". We all have the double helix of the human condition, our "spiritual DNA", being both good and evil.

Only God is good and has the single DNA of goodness without any evil whatsoever. Even as Christians, we can be filled with a multidimensional heart full of all sorts of motives. We may have a pure motive of wanting to help out a stranger in need, but also mixed in with it we want to be seen by others as a "compassionate" person.

We have dual motives. Probably everything we do in life has more than one motive. We feed our faces to nourish our bodies as well as to satisfy our cravings and appetites. Some good, some bad and some probably neutral.

At any rate, it is a godly trait to be single hearted, motivated only with good intentions. This is where God wants to take our characters- to a place where we only have single, God honoring motives, no selfish or ulterior ambitions. But how many of us are there yet? I know I've not arrived. I've set that as a prominent goal in my life.

Anyways, I went in circles with the broken heart syndrome and loneliness consuming me. I sometimes prayed and cried out to God all night that He would allow me to find a woman of God to share my life with and to have a son and daughter. I mean, I literally wept for hours and pleaded with God to take away my loneliness. Many times He came through and I was good to go for about 6 to 12 weeks with a pure, single-hearted devotion to God. However, another beautiful Christian girl who could potentially be "The One" would ruin me all over again. I would relapse into loneliness and self pity.

God himself said, "It is not good for man to be alone" so I had a scripture to shove in the face of God... and boy, did I shove it!

Sometimes I would complain, hoop and hollar at God, blaming Him for my deformed fingers as the sole reason that I couldn't get the girl of my dreams. I can't count the many times I tried to manipulate the heart of God, as a mere worm of a man, that I could actually succeed in putting a "guilt trip" on the Almighty. We all probably do it or have done it at some point in our lives. We have a need or want and we start praying our pity tears. It's the ol' "I'm suffering here God, don't you care about me?" thingy. We want to tell God that as He sits snugly up in Heaven surrounded by angels and paradise, we are down here being neglected, abused and in real pain.

We forget in that moment that Christ actually came down and took upon Him all of humanity's suffering and sorrow to make a way for us to be eternally saved in that snuggly Heaven by and by.

ECHO: THE SECRET TO WHY WE SUFFER
(What I Learned When I Was Beaten To A Bloody Pulp)

Yes, I have suffered a little in my life from before I was even born, when Mama tried to abort me. Then again when I was born with multiple birth defects. In my childhood, growing up in very abusive and dysfunctional family situations, I was bullied and beaten up because of my hands… even as an adult in many ways… but I can't say that my suffering has been so great that I've become an expert on the subject.

We all suffer greatly in some way, even those born to wealth and royalty. But grasping why we suffer and the great sufferings of humanity is always an intriguing subject, especially in light of the fact that there is a God of love who is behind all of creation. Sometimes it's hard to marry those two ideas. But something happened to me that forced me to confront God on the subject face to face.

After YWAM, I was working as a missionary with a ministry down in Houston, Texas called His Touch Ministries. It was a halfway house for drug addicts and homosexuals who had contracted the HIV virus and expressed a desire to change their lifestyles to serve God. The ministry had been given a multimillion-dollar home that just happened to be in a neighborhood that had declined rapidly into poverty and decadence.

The home was very nice and accommodating and really was a wonderful fit for the ministry. However, it was smack dab in the center of this drug and gang infested neighborhood. This didn't bother me, for I have always loved the quote by Charles Thomas Studd, *"Some wish to live within the sound of church or chapel bell; but I want to run a rescue shop within a yard of hell."* Actually, both my brother Sean and I came on board with this ministry because we saw that it truly was an active rescue shop within a yard of hell.

We lived there at the home ministering to these sad, totally mixed up and broken men who desperately needed Jesus. Some of them where spiritually attuned to this fact; others were just using the ministry as a flop house to crash between their sin filled partying and riotous living. But it was okay because we wanted to reach them as well.

I felt I was really just there to be a light and to show them the love of Jesus.

I was much younger and much more naïve (which is a nice diplomatic term for ignorance), naïve in my understanding of my own faith in the Lord, the world, the devil and the principles of spiritual light versus spiritual darkness. So I had this false concept in my understanding that since I was in ministry, working for God and trying to be a light to the darkness, that I had an invincible shield around me. I presumed that I had two giant guardian angels at my right and my left at all times. God was my bodyguard and being a "King's kid", I could walk fearlessly and boldly around this very dangerous neighborhood with no problem.

Well, to make a long story short, I was mugged one night by two young men, pistol whipped until they fractured my skull and left me a bloody pulp out in the middle of the street. I really think they had intended to rob me and then kill me but a few cars had gone by.

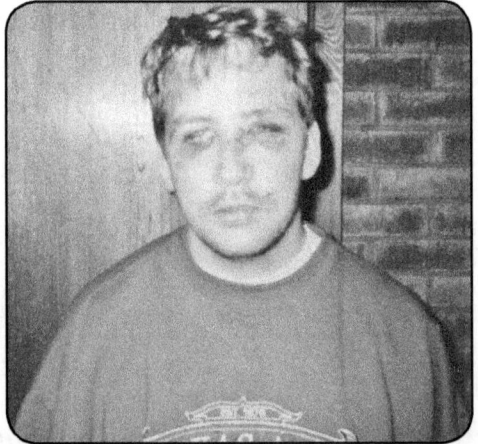

Recovering From My Brutal Attack

One lady actually rolled down her window and reasoned with them to leave me alone. Too many witnesses had made them stop their murderous plan, I think. Or it could be that the Holy Spirit convicted any conscience they had left, because as they were beating me, I remember telling them over and over, "Please don't do this, Jesus loves you." At any rate, I started to blackout and only vaguely remember bits and pieces of wandering the street, knocking on someone's house door, covered in my blood, asking for help. I then vaguely recall paramedics tearing off my pants and shirt and putting me in back of an ambulance.

I did learn a very valuable spiritual lesson from this ordeal, a little secret to why we suffer. I am not so proud to assume I have a complete revelation but I would like to share with you what I do know.

First though, a testimony of a miracle in this ordeal- When I left the hospital a few days later, I had no wallet, money or keys to my car because the night I was mugged I assumed the muggers had taken it all. I prayed that God would help me find at least my keys. I told my friend, "Let's go back to the location where I was mugged, maybe they took my money and threw my wallet and keys on the ground and it's still around somewhere."

My friend looked doubtful but he drove me there. It had steadily rained since the night they had mugged me. I began looking up and down the area and in the tall grass on the side of the road. Amazingly, I found both my car keys and my wallet on the side of the road. And guess what? All the money in my wallet was still there!

The only thing that was totally missing was a little snap cover Bible that I always had in my back pocket. It kinda looked like a fat wallet because of how over the years I had sat on it. I think the muggers were in a hurry or something, in the pitch black dark they might have mistook my Bible as the wallet. I had basically, in my confused beaten state threw everything at them. I looked and looked for that Bible too but it was nowhere to be found. I wondered if the muggers ran off with it and when they got to a secure location opened it up hoping to find money. I hoped that God had let them read something that convicted their hearts like "Thou Shalt Not Steal."

Anyways after that, I told people I had a "Passing Out Bible

Ministry"… I would pass out and someone would steal my Bible! Smiley face inserted here.

Anyways, when I came back to the ministry from the hospital, for quite a few days during my physical healing, I had an intense spiritual battle going on in my soul. I basically became very depressed and disillusioned in my faith in the Lord. I couldn't understand why God had put a giant hole in my invincible bubble and why my guardian angels seemed to be away on vacation while I was beaten to a bloody pulp.

Yes, I have to admit, I did all the things many of us do when we go through trials and tribulations, I stuck my fist in the air and raged against Heaven. I told God he wasn't fair, or just or a good Father. I am ashamed of it now, but I was pretty ticked off that I was seemingly so neglected by the Sovereign Lord God Almighty... especially since I assumed I was one of His "special children". You know, one of those special children whom God the Father doesn't ever let bad things happen to them?

I was doing God's will, I thought. I mean, isn't there some scripture somewhere in the Bible that plainly says that if you're in the will of God, no bad or traumatic thing will ever happen to you? I searched long and hard for those scriptures but even to this day I have yet to find one. Even if it's not in the Bible, isn't there some unseen spiritual law that clearly says that if you're a child of God, and doing some awesome, one on one intense ministry stuff that God's protection is guaranteed… that no evil will befall us who are most pious and devoted to the Kingdom of God?

So I was disillusioned until I finally simmered down and could hear God's voice above the clamor of my pride and self centered piety. I was confined to my bed so my struggle ended up as a lengthy conversation between God and I. It went something like this-

Heath: "God, I can't abandon my faith or deny your existence altogether, because I know you're real through all the experiences of you in my life. Besides, all creation screams of your benevolent existence… but I am depressed and disillusioned right now about my faith, about you and about doing ministry altogether. I don't know where I am, or who I am, Lord."

God: "I know my son, you are exactly where I want you to be, though.

Heath: "So you want me to be disillusioned and down and out like this?

God: "Yes, my son, I do. Many find jewels of precious truth and the secrets of my Kingdom through their disillusionments. And you will too."

Heath: "Okay… So Father, what might I learn from this course "Suffering 101?"

God: "Well Heath, what does My Word say about suffering in this present time?"

Heath: Well, it's not worth comparing to the glory that will one day be revealed, I guess."

God: "And what else?"

Heath: "Um, well it's supposed to be a light, momentary affliction… but Lord, being beaten and pistol whipped until my skull was broken didn't feel too light to me."

God: "Son, you can't see the forest because of the giant trees just in front you… you can't see the splendor of the panoramic view of my perfect will and divine plan looking through the pinhole of a finite, mortal life. Your vision is limited to what's in your face right now. You reason and react like any man who can't see beyond the here and now. But I behold all of eternity! As my child, I want you to begin thinking long term… like as in forever. I want you to have always before you an eternal perspective."

Heath: "Yes, Lord, I know I can't see even one tenth of one degree in the circumference of the 360 degrees of your eternal view… but Lord, why did you abandon me? Why didn't my guardian angels kick some butt? Did I really have to go through all that pain to learn something?"

God: "Well Heath, you are pretty thick headed. Besides you only gave me a token, insincere thanks that you weren't killed in that ordeal. If I had abandoned you, you'd be talking to me right now before the judgement seat of Christ. And by the way, your angels did kick butt and that's why you're still alive.

Just as you can't truly learn how to swim on dry land or even by reading an illustrated "Swimming For Dummies" book, you can't learn some of the deep eternal truths of my Kingdom without some real experiences to get you there, Heath. Have you not prayed to me many times, 'God give me revelation and deep understanding of your Kingdom?' Do you think that you can just coast along on a flowery path of roses, of comfort and convenience to enter into my Kingdom? When my Word says clearly that it is through much tribulation that my children enter the Kingdom of God?"

Then I hung my head in shame and told God, "Oh. Okay, I'm sorry Father. Even now, I'm starting to see the forest. I shouldn't have charged you with neglect and abandonment. That's just the spoiled kid inside of me. I know you love me and this mugging/beating didn't take you by surprise. If anything, I probably deserve what I got."

But God interrupted my pretentious humility and said, "No Heath, you didn't deserve what you got. You deserved a lot, lot more… but fortunately My Son stepped in and took your punishment by hanging on a cross for you. The suffering you received through this ordeal was not your suffering but it was My Son's! You just happened to be the one they took it out on.

You should understand that to live for Christ is to partake or *"fellowship in His sufferings"*… that the true Christian experience is not a nice, neat, little package of going to church on Sundays, and some token religious exercises you do to feel good about yourself. My Word says, *'Yea, all who desire to live a godly life shall suffer…'*

This is what I meant when I said, *'take up your cross and follow me.'* Your cross is more than a cliché or religious metaphor. It is a life surrendered to dying… to dying daily on the cross where all self righteousness, self centeredness, self worth, self indulgences, self importance, self esteem is crucified, so that my Spirit, my resurrected life can shine through you."

God continued slicing and dicing me on the cutting board of His Word, "The truth is Heath, how can I use you to show the world My kingdom if you react like worldly people do, who have no faith, when trials, tribulations and offenses come? You act as if you are more special or more privileged than the rest of humanity who suffer in like manner. Your ordeal is just one common to all mankind.

Being a believer, being My child does not exempt you from this life's ordeals. It rains on the just and the unjust. It also floods and destroys the just and unjust. However, the just can many times pray away the evil… and miracles can and do happen… but not always. Sometimes, no matter what, if it is your time to go there is no way to circumvent it. But as My child, if you are looking past the here and now with an eternal perspective, death, no matter how it comes, is no grim reaper, but a glad angel to whisk you to your blessed eternal habitations with me, your Lord and Savior.

Do you really believe in me, a just and holy God who is pure love? Do you not think that I will make every wrong, right, every injustice, I will bring to justice? Every moment of suffering in your temporal life, no matter how morbid, horrifying, or painful, it might be, will I not apply a beautiful healing on that day that will leave you completely cured without a single scar to remember your trauma and suffering?

Yes, the only scars that will remain in the everlasting kingdom are the scars upon Me, the lamb of God that took away the sins of the world. I will dry your tears and store them in my bottle. There will be no more sorrow or death! My beautiful children will only be filled with innocence and laughter for all of eternity. I promised you this and I will fulfill my Word!

Yet you doubt me in your trial, in your tribulation.

You think you're innocent, my child? No one is truly innocent. Only My son was innocent. But you think that because you are My child that common calamities should never ever befall you… and when they do… you practically want to give up your faith in me. Heath, you sound more like a "fair weather friend" rather than one of my true friends. If you're going to follow me, follow me to the cross and not to some glamorous unrealistic Christian life, free from pain and sorrow. Because *"in this world, you will suffer tribulation"*, trials and persecution. Evil men and demons will plot to hurt you and take your life. But be of good cheer… Look past the here and now. Look upon eternity… for I have overcome the world! Whatever happens to you in this life, be it small or great, be it trivial or traumatic, be it suffering or even sudden, horrific death, settle it now in your heart that I am on your side and everything that happens to you will ultimately fit within my loving plan to give you an eternal future and hope."

"For I know the plans I have for you," declares the LORD, "plans to prosper you and not to harm you, plans to give you hope and a future." Jeremiah 29:11

Well, after being fried up as a fritter by the spirit of God, it was hard for to me to open my mouth. Yes, believe it or not. The only thing left in me was the question that burns in so many of us. So I said, "Well Lord, when evil befalls us like in my situation, or when some Christian dies in a horrific manner, or even an unbeliever, is it always 'your will' or something you planned as the Sovereign Lord God Almighty?"

The Lord answered me, "No. It hasn't been My will since the fall of Adam and Eve that my children should suffer, that mankind should experience any of the evils of this fallen world. It's not My will that men should murder or that accidents should maim. My will is for a perfect world, a world with no pain, no sorrow, no evil, no sin. But all of mankind's sorrows and sufferings, even your own, are due to the choices you make, either directly by sin and rebellion against my ways or by the consequences thereof. It is by the curse of sin itself, from the fall of Adam to the gradual disintegration of the elements or natural disasters. Most suffering comes by wrong choices from a fallen humanity and the rest are due to a fallen, cursed world in decay. Both are the consequences of sin.

All my children who truly love me, no matter how holy or disciplined in My ways, will never know complete perfection in their flesh, in this world. They are still subject to the elements of this world, to the indiscretions of a fallen nature. They may be 99% of the time walking in My Spirit, but in a brief moment of weakness… even that 1% moment, they turn to the beggarly elements and do a fleshly thing. Perhaps as silly as impatience or road rage in traffic. In the stress of the day, they lose patience and swerve into a lane that ultimately takes their lives or the life of someone else. Could I have prevented that? Many times I do intervene with a miracle. But sometimes not. Did I plan it? Did I want it? Was that a judgment on them? A consequence of choice?

As a loving Father, I never desire men to suffer, ever! The first paradise, the Garden of Eden revealed that… but free will and free choice are part of My character, My image, which man was created in the likeness of. It is not my desire to have robots that choose love because they were made to choose it. Love by its very nature, is given and received as a choice. Never out of manipulation and control but out of an expression of free will.

Ultimately through suffering, those redeemed are going to learn that the way of love is the only way to exist. It is My kingdom. My Son was the ultimate example of love. No man can enter My kingdom without learning this way of love. It is the only way that mankind can exist in eternity. That is why all suffering is temporary and I make use of it as a teacher, as a trainer of men's hearts and souls. This will bring the greatest revelation to the soul. It will eventually make all of redeemed humanity both one with the Father, and one with the Son. All the laws and the prophets can be summed up in the simple choice to love.

As a loving Father, I am committed to this perfection, to this paradise to come. Those who ultimately choose the way of love will reign with me in My kingdom."

As I pondered this revelation, living in a world full of

temptation, trial and tribulation, making a choice to love others, I realized that love is always a sacrifice of self and ironically a suffering of our own soul. To crucify our self love is the beginning of loving others as Jesus loved us. Because human nature without God's love is to be totally selfish. It is the love of self that wants to be the center of attention, that wants to gratify it's fleshly desires, even if it hurts or debases another human being or God. So most of the world, even within the so called Christian mainstream here in America, there is a large focus and emphasis on self love, self pleasure, self comfort, self convenience, gratifying the desires of the temporal flesh in the here and now... with no eternal perspective.

How many of us truly walk in God's love on a consistent basis? Most of us like to talk about ourselves. Or if we're professing Christians, we might spiritually manipulate people into thinking about how great a person that we are, what a fine virtuous Christian, what a great spiritual leader or pastor, etc.

Many pastors and mega church leaders actually promote themselves more than the Lord Jesus they claim to glorify. I have been sometimes flooded with "Christian marketing material" that had the church or ministry leader's faces and names plastered on every page. Their image and name in lights, blown up on billboards and on television screens to promote themselves. I'm not condemning the practice of using our photo or name in publications or broadcasts. Ok, don't take it wrong. However, sometimes it becomes overwhelmingly and awkwardly evident that someone other than Jesus is stealing the limelight in our so called "ministries" and "churches".

This is partly due to America having such a "marketing and advertising" modality in everything. But should the saints of God and the humble servant leaders of Christ be "showy", celebritized and "glamorized? Shouldn't we live above this reproach of worldly fame? Should we not lift up Jesus alone, instead of wanting the praises of men, or worse, filthy money from using "ministry" as sort of a "spiritual prostitution" to build our multi-million dollar ministries? I know some folks will be offended by these questions, but tell me, would the lowly, humble Savior really desire His church leaders to live so extravagant and out of sync with the rest of humanity suffering in a raging sea?

Self-love has deceived many religious souls and they really think they are the hottest thing since John the Baptist. Full of religiosity and spiritual ego, they live in sprawling mansions, drive expensive cars, have private jets to take them to their next "spiritual conference" to milk the naïve and gullible church folks out of their tithes and offerings. All the while, they truly believe they represent this meek, humble, non-materialistic Lord Jesus of the Bible.

To Truly Live, We Must Die

Self-love is the root of man's greatest downfall. Most of the self help, self esteem and "self love" books and teachings on the market, if thrown into the ocean would do all the church and mankind a huge favor. The problem isn't that we need to focus more on ourselves. No, that is the problem from the beginning of the fall of Adam. This is the problem with this last days generation of a complete narcissistic society and culture. As the scripture says, *"In the last days, perilous times will come and men will be lovers of themselves..."* No time in history has self love and sociopathic narcissism been so rampant and problematic in the world. Unbelievable murder, mayhem, debauchery and decadence fills the news these days. Most everyone is living in their own little comfort zone and pleasure bubble yet the world is full of pain and suffering more than ever before. Only a handful of humble people, churches and ministries are actually making a difference in their towns and little communities.

The world is not only going to hell in a hand basket, it's spiraling in free fall towards raw hedonism and Satanic expression. Suffering and sorrow in this world is not to be blamed on the God of love but on the godless love of self. If we all would truly begin to love as Christ taught and loved us, we would begin to find the joy and lasting happiness and peace we all so desire.

I'm not talking about an unhealthy self hatred either. You are to "love yourself" in the sense that you identify your worth and value in God, your Creator. Your life is important and has a very critical part in history or HIS STORY. However, that self esteem, that self confidence resolutely rests in what God thinks of you and not in what mere mortal men think of you, including yourself. This is the healthy and humble self love God desires. In it, we can love others properly.

The happiest people in the world are the most generous and kind, who have developed a habit of esteeming others better than themselves. They are constantly sacrificing their own needs to meet the needs of others. They are knowingly or unknowingly tapping into the very core of God's divine nature and His expressed image.

We were created to be like God, in the image of His likeness. When we fulfill the law of selfless love, we actually are rewarded with a divine joy that is directly connected to God's character. I have met the poorest people who were very rich and I have met the richest people who were very poor. There are countless folks in third world countries who walk barefooted and sleep on a dirt floor but to meet them you would think they were kings living in castles. Their faces glow with an unworldly joy and they have not a materialistic bone in their body. Should you try to give them something of worth, they do not greedily grasp it as their own with a feeling of "this belongs to me now". They will turn around and share it with everyone until the thing is dispersed and consumed by all in need. Amazing selfless love!

I have been challenged and convicted many times by people of this caliber. I have personally come to the conclusion that to be born in America, with our emphasis on materialism and wealth to bring us happiness, is more a curse and not as "blessed" as we think it is. Like the Word teaches in the book of Revelation, *"We are rich and increased with goods and have need of nothing... but truly we are poor, blind, wretched and naked."*

I share now about the love of self versus selfless love because this is key to understanding why we suffer... why suffering and sorrow is so common to our human condition. Why war, murder, mayhem, crime, turmoil and distress of nations is what we read in the headlines everyday. God speaks to his people and says that it is through God's love alone, this selfless love, that we begin to break the cycle of sin, injustice and evil all around us.

When we choose to forgive and have mercy rather than to despise and take revenge upon someone, we choose to look at people around us not with the intent to manipulate them for our own agendas and selfish motives, to use people to get what we want, but we look at every opportunity to try to help people in their need. We try to be an example so that they too can live with a heart of selfless love.

We choose to respect all men and women, boys and girls with decency and true spirituality rather than with debasement, degrading them with sensuality and the lust of the flesh. It is then we can dialog with one another without a spirit of pride and self importance, self religiosity. We can be humble, patient and kind. These are the things which bring healing rather than hurt, good pleasure rather than pain, sweet song rather than suffering.

So why do we suffer? It is mostly because of our own sins against God's spiritual laws that we suffer, through the consequences of such disobedience and rebellion. We cannot get around the consequences of our sins. We will reap what we sow. This is one of God's main spiritual laws fixed in all eternity. Like Billy Graham used to say, *"We can't sow our wild oats and then pray to God for a crop failure!"* God will allow us to suffer the consequences of our sins and wrong choices so that we might learn the way of righteousness, the way of selfless love. It's only then can we enter the Kingdom of God. The good news is, we don't have to wait until we die to enter His kingdom! We can be His kingdom on earth! We can bring His kingdom to others. We can stop the vicious cycle of evil and suffering. We can calm the raging seas around us. This is why Jesus wants to be the Lord and Savior of our lives. This is why He commands us to repent and change our ways.

So there you have it, in a nutshell. I must confess that it's harder to walk out selfless love on a daily basis than to explain it academically to you as I have now. I fail miserably many times as my "self", my ego, my flesh is that "fly in the ointment". But it is my desire to live like my Lord. It is my greatest desire to one day be completely free of the love of self and to fully walk as Jesus walked. I think this is the litmus test to those who have been born again by the Spirit of God. It is not that our natures have completely transformed into perfect, selfless characters in this world. I truly wish that were possible. But we want that with all our hearts, and we do press on to that goal to be holy, to be pure of evil, to love selflessly, to forgive readily.

The Bible says **"Those who have this hope of Christ in them purify themselves even as He is pure." John 4:4** We may not be perfect, but we are striving with all our hearts to walk this walk of faith and holiness that was once delivered up to the saints. And if we sin, if we fail, we do not wallow in the sewers of self pity and self justification for our sins, we immediately repent, get back up, beg for God's mercy and once again "strive to enter the kingdom of God", to be the sanctified vessels of honor, fit for the Master's use.

It is those who wallow in their sins and even splash around in amusement of them, that I have a very hard time believing they have ever been touched by God's love, or experienced the true joys of His holy kingdom. I think they are deceiving themselves.

A real quick story that illustrates entering into the kingdom of God by choosing to love… It actually has to do with my precious mother when I was beaten to a bloody pulp.

After a few weeks of God healing me both physically and spiritually from the ordeal, I went to see my Mama. She was a fairly new Christian then. Even before she was a Christian she was a very loving and forgiving person. She actually was one of the best examples I knew of someone who forgave quickly and quite thoroughly. She forgave a lot of great injustices in her life that most people would be embittered about to their very grave. But not Mama, she was a forgiver.

Except the time when I visited her after being beat up. She told me, almost in tears "Heathy, I can't forgive those boys for doing that to you; I just can't!" She was my Mama and I was her baby boy. I think I chuckled at her and told her "Mama, you have to forgive them. I already have and we must never allow a root of bitterness to spring up in us. The world is always going to be there to try to put a bitter splinter between us and God and we can't allow it. God will take care of those boys but we must pray for mercy." My Mama just shook her head no and we got on to some other subject.

Ever so often, during the next few months, she would remind me that she hadn't forgiven those boys. I would encourage her to let it go and let God in.

Then one day she called me on the phone and she was crying. I said "What's wrong Mama?" She replied, "Today, I forgave those boys. I forgave them Heathy, from my heart and I prayed for them to be saved!" I rejoiced with her for that breakthrough! She had learned the law of love and in that moment she again entered the kingdom of God! What was a stumbling block to her faith became a stepping stone to victory. The suffering that could have made her a bitter person, through Christ made her a better person.

I want to challenge all of us, to not try to answer academically, the question "If God is good, why is there suffering in this world?" Instead, let us answer that question by living according to the God of love and His holy Word, by being the answer to that question, to live without the love of self... to do as Jesus called all His true disciples to do in Matthew chapter 16 verse 24 *"If any man wants to come after me, let him deny himself, and take up his cross, and follow me."* The way of Christ is the way of the cross. It's the crucifixion of self love so that we can be resurrected to a new life of God's love and holiness. May this truth go deep into the inward parts of all who hear what the Spirit of God is speaking. The secret to why we suffer is that God, our Father, in His wisdom and love, will always choose the best path to bring us into a revelation of His love. He uses our sins and the consequences of them to discipline us until the light bulb finally turns on in our awareness... that if we obey the single law of love, we do not need to be governed by or forced to obey any other law in the whole universe! We will have "arrived". This is the single greatest revelation and truth that God so desires men to comprehend and live by in the raging sea.

I still do not fully understand why we suffer in this world as we do, or why God seems not to answer every prayer with a pentecostal miracle. But I know God is good and He will make every wrong right. He will take away every pain and the tears from our eyes in the end. This fact alone should be enough to sustain us through the dark and suffering days each one of us will undoubtedly face in this fallen world, in this raging sea.

ECHO: GOD ANSWERS PRAYERS
(Even The Ones We Don't Deserve)
Really? Really.

I can say without hesitation, God has answered and been faithful to me in every prayer I have ever prayed. Yes, I cried out for years, since the age of 18 to the age of 35 that God would bless me with a wife, a daughter and son. I remember praying exactly this. I wanted to be married. I wanted a son and daughter.

As a Christian, I wish I could testify that I had become "SUPER CHRISTIAN" over the years. But alas, my process of redemption and sanctification has always been a slow and tedious one... for me and for God, I'm sure. Through the 90's and into the first years of the new millennium, I battled this loneliness and the raging sea of emotions and demons that attacked me as a single person. Only my Mama knew how lonely I felt at times. Yes, I loved God and knew He was there but I was like Adam without his Eve.

My Beautiful Bride, Marivania

Finally, after 17 years of self centered anguish and thrashing about in a raging sea all alone, God gave me a beautiful wife. It was a pure miracle to find Marivania, a gorgeous Brazilian girl, full of love for God and people. When I proposed to her, God had given me Proverbs 31 that morning, as the scripture refers

139

to a woman of Godly character. After she accepted to marry me, I spoke with her about the scripture. Then we drove to a store to pick up some food. I unintentionally parked next to a car that had PRVBS31 as the license plate number. I didn't really need confirmation about Marivania but God gave it to me anyways. I guess since He knew I had a habit of second guessing myself and sometimes sabotaging good things He confirmed it to me in many ways.

It was after our wedding that Mama passed away just a few months later. I have looked back and seen the hand of God always working in my life. He allowed me to marry Marivania just in time before He took my mother home. The devastation of losing my Mama was so much lessened by having a beautiful wife at my side, who loved God and me.

Jordi, Mama And Proud Daddy

During Christmas that same year, we had the memorial service for Mama. Marivania was very sick during this time, but she tried to hide it as much as she could from me and my grieving family. We found out later that she was sick because she was pregnant. Jordanna Victorya Goodman, my beautiful baby girl was born in September of 2003.

So many miracles and God's provision during those months where we had very little resources and finances. I could write a book just about that.

Five years came and went and life was good with Marivania and my little girl in pigtails, "Jordi-Pants".

One day Jordanna said to me, "Daddy I want a puppy and a little brother."

"Well, Jordi, I don't know about both a puppy and a little brother. What do you want more?" I asked.

Jordanna thought for a second and said, "I want a little brother more."

As a father, I really wanted to somehow bring Jordanna to a place where she could "see that God exists" in reality and not just some invisible man that we pray and sing to. I wanted her to somehow experience the power of God's love and His divine providence in our lives.

I had talked to my wife on many occasions about having another child, but of course, she being the nine month vessel God would have to use, it was left to her choosing... and she made an emphatic "no" every time the subject was brought up. I kept hinting but ultimately to live considerately with my wife, I wanted it to be her choosing. Jordanna was privy to some of these "second child" conversations and she would side with Daddy and tell Mommy that she wanted a sibling too. So after Mama made her very firm "no" known to us both, we secretly conspired against her in a wonderful way.

I told Jordanna that God would honor her prayer if she prayed specifically for what she wanted. This way she could learn that God answers specific prayers. To be honest, she vacillated between a puppy and a baby brother at first, but soon became convinced that a baby brother would be a better playmate. So for about a year, Jordanna would pray for a baby brother.

During this time, Jordanna and I would talk as if he was already a part of our family. We already named the baby "Joshua" and talked as if he already existed. So much so that Mama would fuss at Jordanna and me for "talking nonsense". So secretly, I told Jordanna that if God was going to answer this prayer for a baby brother, He would have to first soften Mama's heart concerning wanting a second child. So we both tag teamed on praying that Mama's heart would change. Then one day it happened, out of the blue and after many emphatic "no's", Mama whispered, "Let's try to have another baby."

It was then I knew the hard part was done. Joshua was as good as born. Well, a few months later Mama became pregnant and Jordanna was incredibly excited about becoming a big sister. We, of course, would have been equally joyful if God had seen fit to give us another daughter and Jordanna, a sister... but inwardly, I had always prayed and dreamed of someday having a son. I also knew that Jordanna's specific prayer was for a baby brother. So there were many times during the pregnancy leading up to knowing the gender of our baby that I told Jordanna to keep praying for what she wanted specifically and so did I.

Well, to our happy amazement, God was faithful to give us what we had specifically desired. All that time of talking about Joshua even before he was a twinkle in Mama's eye finally paid off. And God spared two birds with one worm. He taught me that

Jordi, Daddy & Mama Celebrating Joshie!

the Father wants to fulfill any wholesome, God honoring dream that any one of us might have. He taught my daughter that God really listens, acts and answers specific prayers.

I thanked my God for Marivania, Jordanna and Joshua and the lesson I learned of the incredibly good Father He is in answering my prayers to have a little family of my own... so specifically and so undeserved.

ECHO: STING OF DEATH
Do You Believe This?

I want to share about my Mama and her last days in this world.

My mother was the world to me. After my conversion, besides the One Who Died For Me, she was a rock and fortress to my raging, sea-battered soul. Even though Mama still drank and smoked and had not yet converted to Christ, she was an anchor that I knew was there for me in the raging sea. I truly hope we all have a loved one like that. If not, you can still know that kind of love through Jesus.

Soon enough though, the Lord began touching Mama's heart. She gave up drinking all together and slowly changed over the years into a woman of God. One of her greatest struggles was her addiction to cigarettes. The raging addiction held on for many, many years. Yet, as she walked with God, she began transcending the raging sea. One day, Mama braved the storm and used nicotine gum to help her slay the smoking dragon. Jesus doesn't mind if we cheat a bit as long as we're going in the right direction.

Mama told me, "Heathy, God spoke to me and said that if I gave up smoking that I wouldn't die from cancer." For Mama, Jesus became her greatest motivation and her greatest support.

Yet, still far from perfect, Mama still had to deal with a great raging sea within her and around her. She was a "worry wart" and could easily stress out at sometimes the smallest of things, but she was growing. My step-dad, Marvin had mellowed out as well. He too was going to church and seeking after God. Yet they battled against their own flesh and with each other in the raging sea. As time went on I could see more and more of my Savior's love in Mama.

Mama always feared death and dying before she had

143

become a Christian. She especially feared cancer. Every time we talked and the subject somehow got on death or dying, Mama would speak about her fears. I began to pray for Mama about this. I wanted Mama to overcome her fear of death and dying, especially since she had become a Christian. I would pray, "Jesus take the fear out of her. Give her peace and let her know you are going to be with her always, especially in death."

One of the most awesome revelations in this life as you begin to brave the raging sea with God is that Jesus came down to earth to identify with us. Through him we can vanquish the fear of death forever in our lives! *"Jesus himself became like them and shared in their humanity. He did this so that through His death He might destroy the Devil, who has the power over death, and in this way set free those who were slaves all their lives because of their fear of death." Hebrews 2:14-15* Of course, not having the fear of death shouldn't make us somehow inclined to eagerly walk out in front of a speeding mac truck. We respect life in the raging sea, but our great hope in Christ keeps us from the fear of death and dying.

Some people think that as a Christian, our faith would kick into overdrive. We would no longer fear death or anything for that matter. For some of us this may be true, but we can't judge others by our own personal experiences with God. Every person who comes to faith in the Master is different. Different raging seas, different enslavements, different tragedies and heartaches that shape us into the darkened souls we become before Christ. However, when the Master takes over our lives, He begins the process of redemption and sanctification within us. No one living is ever perfected in an instant. Each man has his own sins, demons and weaknesses to overcome. But the God of mercy sees when our hearts have stopped loving sin, when our souls have stopped enjoying evil pleasures.

He sees when our hearts become filled with regret, remorse and repentance. Jesus wants us to relinquish everything to Him. The sooner we do, the sooner the healing begins. Many ragamuffins come to God still chained to certain elements, still enslaved to a past with haunting fears, recurring sin, failures and demons. But the Master is patient, loving and merciful. He waits for us as a Father lovingly waits for a son who slowly must put down, one by one, a pile of worthless rocks that he holds so tightly to his chest. As the son releases the rocks, he experiences more and more of the freedom that comes from walking in the ways of God.

Until all the rocks are gone and Father and child embrace in a moment of true intimacy and heartfelt trust, there will be a raging sea to conquer. All of us are like this and can only know a limited freedom and limited spiritual rest as long as we live in this fallen world. Mama was a ragamuffin "rock collector" like us all, but she slowly let go of her rocks. She was growing into a beautiful daughter of God.

So when she was diagnosed with lung cancer, with no viable treatment options at the hospital in Abilene, Texas in December of 2002, I drove all the way from Georgia to be with her. It seemed like God had failed her. I remembered her child-like faith to believe she wouldn't die of cancer and now this? Here she had COPD (Chronic Obstructive Pulmonary Disease) and now lung cancer with perhaps months to a few years to live... I just knew she would be so fearful, devastated and worried.

When I came to her bedside, her eyes lit up with a fiery warmth of love, as they lit up for all her children and grandchildren. "Heathy, you made it!" Mama was so happy to see me and she seemed not as devastated as I had imagined she would have been.

The next morning, I took my precious Mama out of the hospital and we started our drive from Abilene to Blanket, Texas.

We listened to the radio and the song "I Can Only Imagine" came on. She turned it up and said, "This is my favorite song of all time!" I agreed. We listened together and even sang to it. After the song ended, Mama and I began talking more openly about her lung cancer diagnosis. I encouraged her that God was going to heal her and that we could beat the cancer with faith, and also perhaps a more radical health regimen and alternative herbal remedies that I had read about.

I asked her outrightly, "Mama, are you afraid?"

She looked at me with all sincerity. "No Heathy, I am not afraid... I'm not afraid to die at all. I know where I'm going... I just fear how I am going to die... how I might suffer and all."

"No worries, Mama, I don't believe God is going to take you by way of lung cancer. I refuse to believe that!"

I held my Mama's hand. "Besides, I have prayed many times for you Mama, that when God calls you home to be with Him that you would fall asleep one night and wake up in the arms of Jesus! I know God is going to honor my prayer."

Mama squeezed my hand as her reply to my comforting words. "I hope you're right Heathy. I just don't want to become so debilitated and suffer, that's all."

We made it to Ally's home where Mama requested to stay for a while, which my sister gladly accepted. I think Mama didn't want to be alone at all. She wanted to be around her children and grandchildren as much as possible to help cope with her diagnosis and the raging sea within.

Eventually I had to return to Georgia, but I left Mama knowing I would return with my beautiful new wife Marivania for Christmas in just a few short weeks. We would all be together again at Christmas. We would celebrate our Messiah's birth and encourage Mama to fight the good fight.

It was just a few days before Christmas. We were only days from leaving Georgia to make the trip to Texas. I was actually in a health store picking up some herbs and vitamins to take to my mother when I saw Ally's number calling me on my phone. I picked up the phone.

"Hello Ally, what's up?"

"Heath, Mom's dead!"

"Whaaaat?" My heart begin to sink.

"Mom's dead, I can't revive her. She's unresponsive and not

breathing!"

I couldn't believe my ears.

"No, Ally, go over there right now and pray over her and give her CPR!"

"I can't. I tried reviving her! She won't wake up Heath! She's dead... Mom's gone!"

I couldn't accept that. I pleaded with Ally to do all that she could to revive her. The ambulance was apparently on the way. I ended the phone call praying.

Mama Just Weeks Before She Went On Permanent Vacation With Jesus

I prayed so intently that it wasn't so. I commanded life into her body. I prayed for the resurrection power of Christ. But when I called back, the news was the same. Mama was gone. She was really gone.

I called my wife Marivania and drove to our apartment. My mother couldn't die on me. She was my rock, my anchor, the only soul on earth who I knew loved me unconditionally. Perhaps my Mama didn't fear the day she would die, but I knew deep down I had feared that day ever since I was a small child. It was my greatest fear, even as a Christian.

I loved my Mama more than life itself. She was the most loving, forgiving person I knew... and since she had become a Christian, she had become a best friend too. Even though I had moved away from her, I called her all the time and we would talk about Jesus, faith and praying for family members who still did not know or walk in God's love.

I told my wife and hugged her. She was a rock for me too. But mamas can never be replaced. I ran to my office where I fell on my knees to be alone with God. I couldn't handle the grief. I couldn't bear to think that Mama was really gone, that I would not get a chance to celebrate Christmas with her beautiful, beaming eyes and smiles. I cried intensely. My whole body shook just like when my father died.

Now she was gone. Both Mama and Dad were gone. I could not use them as anchors in my raging sea. I cried out to God, "Father, Jesus, Holy Spirit, I need you this hour. I need you to be with me! I need you to show me the way. How can I bear the sting of death? How can I endure what my own soul has most feared... a day when I would be alone without my Mama to call, to hear her loving, encouraging voice tell me that she was proud of me, that she was praying for me."

As I knelt there in my office, I grabbed my Bible. In my tears, I demanded God to speak to my soul in that grief stricken, overwhelming lonely moment. I felt abandoned. I needed to know for certain that my greatest rock of all, my Lord and God was still with me, and that my Mama was home safe with Him.

I just randomly opened up the Bible not knowing what passage of scripture it would land on. I would begin to read through my tears. My eyes crash landed on the first scripture that leapt from that beautiful page.

It was John 11:25-26!!!

"Jesus said to her, I am the resurrection, and the life: he that believes in me, though he were dead, yet shall he live: And whoever lives and believes in me shall never die. DO YOU BELIEVE THIS?"

The words pierced through the thick black cloud of grief and anguish of my soul, like a lighthouse beaming through the fog and storm of the raging sea.

How coincidental was that? No, it was another awesome God-incidence! One that I very much needed at that moment to calm the raging sea within me. I just wept on the floor, clutching my Bible. With tears falling upwards I responded to God's Word. "I do believe this, Jesus. I do! Thank you for giving me the only word that could soothe the sting of death. I love you Jesus, I love you so much!"

Oh death where is your sting? Where is the haunting loss?
Now that I have known the resurrection beyond the painful cross?
I may not be sure of many things in this stormy, raging sea... But I
do know the lighthouse that breaks the darkness inside of me.

Papa God sent an angel to make sure I opened my Bible to that exact scripture, at that exact moment. As soon as I read it, the raging sea ceased to have a grip on me. Yes, I still grieved. I still felt loss. But it was not the same. From that moment on, I knew Mama was on vacation with Jesus. God had sent me a postcard from paradise, via His Word to let me know that she was okay, she was safe in Heavenly habitations.

As I wept there, I wept with such intensity and hope. Especially when Holy Spirit helped me realize that God had not failed either my Mama nor me in that hour! As a matter of fact, He kept His promise to her. She had not died from cancer. It was in it's infantile stage and Mama hadn't begun to even suffer from the disease. She had died from a slow but fatal restriction of oxygen from her COPD as she slept that night, which caused her to go into systemic heart failure.

Most incredibly, God had also answered my prayer down to the very exact detail! My Mama just fell asleep that late December night and woke up in the arms of Jesus... just as I had prayed and comforted her with, only weeks earlier! God was so faithful to take Mama like that and keep her from a fearful or painful death experience.

We drove to Texas and the whole family grieved during what was suppose to be a a time of celebration. That Christmas was filled with a mix of emotion and pain. A Christmas tree had scattered gifts but the lights did not glow with warmth. Mama, the raggedy but consistent lifeboat of our family, the hub, was now gone. It felt like my whole family was thrashing in a raging sea of darkness and gloom, but hope was there as well. We held a memorial service for her at the Church of the Lord Jesus and it was a bit surreal. On one hand we mourned, but on the other hand we celebrated, even weeping and clapping with a standing ovation to the Lord God Almighty, the one we knew had faithfully taken Mama home. Death is a powerful reminder that we are mortal, fragile beings in a terrible raging sea... but hope in the living Christ makes it bearable. We can transcend death's ugly, dreary prospect and know real peace and joy as we fight to stay afloat in this raging sea. There is a God and He loves us! He has conquered death to give us eternal life in Him! DO YOU BELIEVE THIS?

ECHO: EVEN ABOUT THE LITTLE THINGS

As I previously said, my Mama was a worry wart and sometimes stressed out about little and even silly things. She unfortunately passed that spiritual DNA down to me. Even as a Christian with lots of faith in God, we can all succumb to being rattled or stressed out at times.

It is partly due to this age we live in, this culture of instant gratifications and the instant results we expect. When we don't get what we expect, we get impatient or we fall apart so quickly to lash out at loved ones. It is an age of anxiety and an over pampered generation. I myself must fight the raging sea in this regard. I am quite certain that some have acquired sainthood concerning never being stressed or anxious about anything but I have yet to arrive. Just ask my wife and kids. No, don't! But I am getting better and closer to my goal.

One autumn day I realized I had lost my wedding band. This wedding band was more than just a symbol of my love and commitment to Marivania. It was the wedding band that had a very sentimental attachment concerning the circumstances of how and why I had it for so long, even years before I was married. Another story for another time.

Jordi & Joshie 2013

I searched for the ring everywhere in the house. I was frantically looking, pulling out couch pillows, scouring toy bins and looking down drain pipes. I think I searched for almost an entire day.

Eventually, after having exhausted almost every conceivable place, I thought I must have lost it on a recent trip we had taken to Tennessee, in a log cabin we had stayed at. I was so stressed out about it that I was literally and physically becoming sick over it.

I finally went to God, whom I should have gone to in the first place.

I basically surrendered it to God. I told God, "Jesus, you know exactly where that wedding ring is and what it means to me. If you want me to get it back then you will let me find it. I am finished looking for it. I place it totally in your hands now. I will not look for it again. If it's your will for me to never get it back, I will accept that too. It's just a thing."

After praying this, I never once looked for it again. I truly left it in God's hands.

About two or three days later, I had to go to work one morning and I was rushing out of my house. Joshua was just a munchkin of a toddler and he came to the door to see me off. It had rained and the front yard was a mess of puddles, mud and grass. Joshua had a little ball in his hand and he threw it off the front porch. I saw the ball land in the front yard in a muddy, traffic area.

I sighed, "Joshie, I'm sorry. Daddy can't play with you right now. I gotta go to work for a little while." I jumped from the car to quickly retrieve the ball and give it back to my son who was standing there wanting it back. As I grabbed the ball, underneath where the ball had landed, a sparkle from a metal object seemed to beam out from the muddy ground. I pushed the mud and grabbed the object. It was my wedding ring!!! It had been almost totally buried in the mud and just a few days or foot stomps later, the ring would have probably been lost forever! Literally, God used my son Joshua, a ball and perhaps a few wet, muddy angels to show me that He cares even about the little things. God loves us so much!

Cedar Lake, Chester Connecticut

ECHO: ON CEDAR LAKE

I could write about so many experiences of God's faithfulness and His reality in my life, but I won't download it all on you. However, to sort of conclude this book's testimony, I want to share the solid faith I have in my Lord.

You see, when I have left the limitations of this physical reality, when death has released me from my exoskeletal shell, and I have transcended forever the raging sea all around me, the angels of this great transition will guide me first to the love of my life, my Lord and Savior Jesus, to gaze upon His beautiful face.

In this life, as I have beheld ever so slight glimpses of Him, I have been changed so dramatically, so absolutely toward His visage. But on that day, at one instance of seeing Him in the fullness of His glory, then all the raging seas that may still linger in the deepest depths of my soul will be forever made tranquil. "Peace be still!" My Savior speaks and it is so. I know I will be eternally changed, repurposed into the child of pure light and love for oneness with Papa God.

I imagine my loved ones gone before me, redeemed by His mercy also, will be standing next in line to welcome me into eternal habitations.

I will look for my earthly father. Jesus will smile and say, "Go through this portal of light... your father is there waiting for you, Heath."

I will go forward and instantly the speed of light will transport me to Cedar Lake, just as it was in my fond memories with my father long ago.

My father will be there at the end of the little pier with a sailboat much like the one we sailed on as children.

When the light of our eyes first meet, we will instantly know the peace of our Lord. There will be nothing there but extreme love and respect for one another. I imagine my father smiling with a pure smile without a hint of the sarcasm, bitterness and pain that once marred his countenance from the raging sea.

"My eldest beloved son, Heath! The Master gave me heads up that you would be here today!" I will notice something familiar about my father. It will be the same sweet, fiery love in his eyes as that of my Savior. All His children will have it.

"I know how you enjoyed being out on the lake Heath, so I prepared for you to sail with me today."

I will walk up to him in his glorified body, free from Diabetes, free from all sickness and deformities and yet his beard fully intact. He will stretch out his arms, "It's been a little while, but I've been saving one of my signature bear hugs just for you Heath." We will embrace, laugh and weep for the joy of that moment. The tears that flow will dissolve any scars that remain.

"Dad, I love you and I just want you to know that it was partially your changed life that helped to change mine!"

My Dad will let out a chuckle. "Well, Son, I wish it were so, but whatever you saw in me back then must have been Jesus, because I was still a ragamuffin, raging sea of sorts, in those weary days. But I know what you mean son, and Jesus answered your prayer. He told me what you had prayed at my passing in your mother's home. Remember, Jesus has innumerable angels as messengers at his beckoning."

We will climb aboard the sailboat and Dad will begin

to work the sails. We will sail with the summer breeze on our backs in the light of God presence, with red pines and great oaks towering around, reflecting in the water that surrounds the little lake.

At some point, we will both take the sails and play tug of war with the forceful wind. I will joke, "You know Dad, Jesus told us that there would be days like this..."

"But here on the New Earth, I thought everything would be so perfect?" My father will reply with a smile and a wink.

"Well Dad, 'Smooth sailing never made skillful sailors!'" I will interject.

My father's eyes will light up brighter. "Hey, that's one of my favorite sayings too! I guess in paradise, we're still learning and growing... or maybe Jesus is just keeping us on our toes, what do you think?"

"I don't know Dad... maybe... but this is Cedar Lake and not the Tranquil Sea, so we might have to push on through here."

Together, Dad and I will work the sails. We will talk and laugh without concern for time, knowing eternity means we don't have to rush to another appointment or worry about a schedule. Time has ceased. I imagine at twilight we will both almost blurt out in unison, "Let's rendezvous with Sean. Jesus just whispered to me that he's waiting at the pier!"

In the distance we'll see another glorified ragamuffin standing at the pier waiting for us.

Sean's eyes will meet Dad's and mine. We will all smile as Dad yells out, "There's my other Pickle Kid!" Sean will climb aboard our little sailboat and another forever in a moment will commence between the three of us. Perhaps my other brothers from my father will join us as well, John and Peter.

Soon enough, after we have exhausted our conversations, our silence of happy fellowship on the water, we will begin to crave the missing link between us all.

The yearning for Jesus will enrapture all of our inner beings and without hesitation Jesus will appear on the sailboat. Our

155

beautiful Master is always with us. "Got room for one more?" He will ask, and we will laugh and cry together, knowing that a complete and perfect redemption of father and sons has taken place in the New Earth... on Cedar Lake.

Every soul who puts their faith in Christ will have their own restoration moment in the age to come. You will get your chance with your Mama, your Dad, your brother, sister or best friend... where failed relationships will be restored, where all pain, resentments and regrets will dissolve, all bad memories forever erased. In a moment, in a twinkle of an eye, peace and joy will rise up in paradise with all the sons and daughters of God. Whoever it may be that needs to heal together with you, God will be sure you will have your moment... on your own "Cedar Lake".

ECHO: TEN THOUSAND YEARS

I have a vision of how it might be ten thousand years after I've fought my raging sea to the end and passing to the other side, transcending all that wearied and warred against my soul to be with my Lord and Savior Jesus.

I imagine a beautiful New Earth where all the children of God, having been restored, are dancing and celebrating barefoot in the fields of Zion, under the light of Yahweh's countenance. I imagine an eternity where there is no pain or sorrow. I imagine a Creator endlessly creating new and beautiful things, making His precious children custodians over all the wonders He performs.

It is there that I will be celebrating love and life with all the redeemed.

An archangel, tall and mighty, will come to my little cottage by the sea (not my other real estate property, my mansion in the City of God). His name is Barachiel, Messenger Of Blessing and he will knock on my door.

Knock Knock.

"Yes, I'll be right there." I open the door and standing there is my good, winged friend.

"Heath, Child of the Most High, It is I Barachiel. Remember today is your day exclusively with the Master. Today is your Solitude Day!" The beautiful archangel smiles with exuberance. "Such a powerful majestic angel and yet so humble and serving," I think to myself.

"Yes, I am so excited to be with the Master. Where are we to meet today?" I inquire.

"He wants to meet you here at your cottage by the Eternal Tranquil Sea. He wants to walk with you along Zion's shore. He will be here just before the twilight hours so be ready, okay?"

"Yes, thank you Barachiel. I will be ready. Thank you my dear friend for reminding me... even though I should have a perfect memory here, right?"

Barachiel winks and turns to walk away. Swoosh, a puff of sparkly white light trails behind as he disappears on another messaging mission. Angelmail is way more glorious than email! Try it sometime through prayer!

In a moment just before twilight, the Master appears at my door. I've been waiting so excitedly, so longing to have my solitude with Him and Him alone. Now He stands dressed in a fine burgundy and white robe with his sandals. He is smiling and His eyes are filled with humility and a fiery love.

"My Lord, you're here! I have been looking forward to our time of solitude. I can't believe ten thousand years has past. With no clocks and no calendars here it's easy to forget the years, decades, centuries and millennial ages!" I spark.

Jesus reaches forward to give me a giant bear hug. I see the beautiful hands of the Master, still scarred from where the nails held Him on the cross. I grab and kiss those beautiful hands.

"Heath, I've been so looking forward to being with you today in the solitude as well. I know we see so much of each other at the banquets, festivals, the councils and at corporate worship of Father, but my time with you in the solitude is very special and precious to me." Jesus speaks with tender enthusiasm and continues, "Let's go walk near the Eternal Tranquil Sea. I have so much to share with you and we can talk on the way."

In a flash it seems, we reach the sea, a beautiful ocean of blue water, much like the Old Earth but without storms or dark raging waters. The waters still crashed majestically on the shoreline and on the rocks but it is quite serene and peaceful. The twilight hour mimics the sunrises and sunsets of the Old Earth too. Here there is no sun, only the Father's brilliant presence. In the twilight, it is not that the Father withdraws His presence, but He allows for a softer evening light of love to settle on the horizon, to give it the same sort of feel as the Old Sun, but much more beautiful and breathtaking. The sky lights up with unimaginable pastel colors and patterns from the Father's creativity. Everyone loves every moment of Zion, but there is something special about the twilight hours.

As the Master and I walk along the shore, the seagulls and Partagolos, a new creation of God, hint their presence with their ambient worship to Father in the background.

"Heath, I love your ideas at the New Earth Council meetings. We love that you are so creative in how to manage some of Father's new creations and your input is so refreshing." The Master's warmth is so incredible.

"You really think so Jesus? I know I can sometimes overthink things and give all of you a laugh or two."

"Yes, sometimes you do but that's okay... we'd rather you overthink than underthink!" Jesus chuckles.

I laugh too.

"I'm quite sure I underthink compared to you," I spark.

"Well, no worries. The Father loves it that all His children are part of the creative process and creative solutions."

"I know He does. I love Father. This reality is so incredibly more than I could ever fathom on the Old Earth," I blurt.

The Master nods, then suddenly stops and points at a good sized seashell near a rock. "Heath, isn't that seashell the one I gave you when you first arrived?"

I peer down the shoreline. "Yes, it is Jesus. That's my place at the Tranquil sea and my Stone Of Remembrance with my new name on it."

As we walk and talk, we finally come upon it. "Take your seashell Heath and put it to your ear," Jesus softly grins and winks.

I put the seashell to my ear.

"What do you hear my friend?" Jesus speaks softly.

"I hear.... I hear faint echoes of the raging sea." I pause and reflect.

"Does it at all hurt you to remember your struggle on the Old Earth?" Jesus looks intently at me.

"No, not at all.. but I know you know this already," I exclaim.

"Humor me anyways" Jesus smiles.

I speak so freely with my Lord. "The eternal weight of glory that I experience now with you and Father has swallowed up all the sorrow and pain... of that brief moment of my initial existence on the old Earth. Even after one minute of being here in Zion, I had almost completely forgotten about it. Now after ten thousand years... well, I would say it's not even a blip on my radar! All my struggles, trials and temptations in the raging sea are as my little brother Sean used to say 'a lifetime of pain will seem less than a mosquito bite compared to eternity.' Compared to my eternal habitation with You and Father now, I can't even remember the raging sea... unless I put this shell to my ear to hear its echoes." I then hand it back to the Master.

"What do you remember most when you hear the seashell?" Jesus asks me as he puts the seashell to His own ear.

"That's easy Jesus. I hear the transcending sound of the beautiful salvation that you worked in me back then. I remember that every heartache, every disappointment, every deep sorrow, every deep sigh of my soul was replaced little by little with your love and grace until it was the only thing that mattered to me. Your love was so amazing back then as it is now, my Lord." I begin to tear up in joyful remembrance.

Jesus tears up too.

"I remember you being a stubborn and ornery ragamuffin soul, Heath. You went around the same mountain a few times and Father had to give you a few love taps, but you came around, didn't you?" Jesus comforts. The Master puts his hand on my shoulder. "I love you Heath. I'm so glad we are here together." Jesus lays the seashell, the stone of remembrance, back in its place.

"I know you love me Jesus, and I would answer back, 'I love you more,' like I used to say to my kids. But it would be a lie, so I won't." I wipe the tears from my eyes.

"Just so we set the record straight, those were tears of joy, Jesus, not tears of sorrow," I chuckle.

"Yes, I know. The sign on the pearly gates reads "No tears of sadness allowed here," Jesus jests.

Jesus stays much longer and we fellowship and talk of the Father's love until the twilight's end.

It is a beautiful Solitude Day with Jesus. At the end of it, we sing together the old hymn, Amazing Grace. How surreal it feels to sing that stanza, "...when we've been there ten thousand years bright shining as the sun, we've no less days to sing God's praise than when we first begun."

I believe all of God's children will one day celebrate and have a Solitude Day with Jesus, perhaps ten thousand years from their own passing over. One day, you too will walk with the Redeemer on the shores of Zion by the Tranquil Sea. You too will remember so slightly, like a wisp of knowing, a hush of remembrance of the raging sea. It won't be a remembrance that brings back pain, resentments or regrets. It will be just a very faint echo of what great salvation was done in you, which will only spark appreciation and love for God's wisdom and grace in your remembering.

God promises to give us all new names, secret names that He has uniquely chosen for us, etched into brilliant stones. *"He who has an ear, let him hear what the Spirit says to the churches. To the one who conquers (the raging sea) I will give some of the hidden manna, and I will give him a white stone, with a new name written on the stone that no one knows except the one who receives it." Revelation 2:17*

I think it could be a seashell to remind us of God's salvation from the sea's hell. I could be way off in left field about this, but it serves me for this book's theme. At any rate, I am sure whatever it is, the raging sea will be no more and, *"Eye has not seen, nor ear has heard, nor has it entered into our hearts, all God has prepared for those that love Him." 1 Corinthians 2:9*

HOW TO TRANSCEND THE RAGING SEA
(The Mother Of All Dad Rants)

I share this message as if it is my last breath upon the earth. For those of you who have read Echoes Of The Raging Sea, it is a testimony of what God has done in my life. I pray that it has created a hunger in you. No, not a hunger that you would want to know more about Heath Christopher Goodman. I am not the main character in it's message. I hope you see that. It truly has been my leading desire and motive to introduce you to Jesus, the true and living Lord and Messiah.

I hope you would want to research more on how you can transcend the raging sea in your own life through Him. I presume you have a raging sea because you live in this fallen world. Perhaps it is more dramatic and horrific as my own testimony. I don't know.

Perhaps you already have faith in Christ to some degree or maybe you've never really called out to Him at all. If you feel you don't have a raging sea in you or around you, then I would love to talk with you and know your secret.

But I know every soul has a raging sea, though some of us may be in denial of it. Jesus said, and I am paraphrasing for the benefit of this theme, ***"These things I have spoken to you, that in me you might have peace (to transcend the raging sea). In this raging sea (this world) you shall have tribulation (crashing waves and moments you feel you are drowning): but be of good cheer (be joyful in knowing this-); I have overcome the raging sea (this world)." John 16:33***

Now as far as my flesh goes, I am walking this earth with no certain timeline and could easily perish at any given moment. So since I am on my proverbial deathbed always, the last message I would want to share is this one.

Yes, the raging sea has you in it's grip. You are struggling in this world like the rest of us, even if you were born with a silver spoon in your mouth. You are thrashing about alongside all of humanity trying to make sense of it all. You see the crashing waves of good and evil, of justice and injustice, of pleasure and pain, of beauty and ugliness, of selflessness and selfishness, of gain and loss, of love and hate. You see it all and depending on the spot you were born and raised into, you experience various aspects of this raging sea.

The first thing that you must do in order to really begin to transcend the raging sea, is to acknowledge that you are not alone in a dark and dismal ocean of meaninglessness. You are not alone with seven billion souls on a lonely planet in a lonely universe. This is a fact you must discover for yourself.

You must take a leap of faith and believe that there is a God, an intelligent, all powerful being who has created all things, whose love and benevolence can be clearly seen by the incredible, artistic beauty of the world He has created.

It's really not that hard to take this leap of faith because the evidence of a divine, loving, intelligent Creator is so overwhelmingly everywhere. It's in the tender, blooming flowers, the colorful diverse creatures of this planet, the majestic mountains, the beautiful lakes, rivers, waterfalls and forests. It's right there staring at you in a mirror... on your cleverly designed face.

Even when you look in the mirror, you can see a highly complex creature with symmetrical eyes, ears, arms and legs with precision design features. The human body itself is a work of incredible ingenuity. When you stare into your own eyeball, do you realize that it is more complex in it's engineering, in its parts and functions than any supercomputer or digital camera available today? If men can intelligently build technology by reverse engineering what they see in nature, in the biological creations of Earth, and that technology is far inferior than the model they took it from, what does that say about our intelligent Creator God? What does that say about intelligent men who would rather deny their Creator's existence than submit to Him?

Did you know that some of the most simple-cell creations of God have more complex parts and functions than that of an Iphone? But we know how absurd it would be to claim an Iphone just randomly constructed itself over billions of years, evolving from inorganic rocks, electrical surges and chemicals crashing into each other. We clearly know the Iphone was created by an intelligent human designer or designers. This is why God says in Romans that everyone of us will all be without excuse on Judgment day, because what He has clearly created unequivocally testifies of His existence, his beautiful character and supreme authority.

When you break through the veil of lies and secular rebellion of taking God out of the equation and inventing myths and fables of "billions of years" of "evolutionary theories", you will have a "eureka moment" when you realize that mere time and random chaotic accidents could have never, ever brought forth the complex, incredible creation around you! No freaking way, Hosea! It's impossible!

Have you ever truly contemplated the vast engineering genius in all of creation or calculated the impossible odds that random accidents just happened to create evolutionary designs and structures that literally show the blueprints of an intelligent designer? Your own DNA, which is literally a deciphered biological, mathematically phenomenal code is proof that there is a God! Billions of years of chaos and accidents didn't create this beautiful harmonious, symbiotic biosphere planet, full of incredible creatures that baffle the most ingenious among us.

The theory of evolution is so debunked by everything we really know and understand! Try to just let go of the programmed indoctrination for just a second and try to look at it with raw logic. Evolution would be like going to a "billion year" demolition derby, and instead of watching old jalopy cars smash and crash into each other towards disintegration and dysfunction, the old, broken down cars instead smashed into each other and suddenly began turning into better cars until enough random accidents through time and space produced a brand new Rolls Royce! It's not even observable science. It's not in line with the known laws of physics or the law of entropy (over time things break down to simpler elements).

The most simple-cell organism (organic) is a Rolls Royce compared to any cosmic dust or rocks (inorganic) that are presumed to have "accidentally" or "randomly" evolved into any sort of supporting elemental/molecular shape or structure.

You want proof that God is real? Just study anything in His creation without bias or a closed minded, atheistic, knee jerk reaction. Once you surrender your willful state of denial to the overwhelming evidence of an intelligent Creator, then you can begin the journey to know Him personally.

So no, you are not thrashing about in a raging sea, full of a chaotic, cosmic accidental humanity, all trying to evolve from the survival of the fittest. You are not a lonely creature without a divine Creator. You are a son or daughter made in the very image of God, the infinitely loving Father! You just happen to be lost in a fallen world that captivates your five senses with lies... until the truth is lost in the overwhelmingly deceptive stimuli of this world. Its broken, demoralized, delusory system overrides your ability to clearly comprehend the truth that is as plain as the nose on your face! Yes, God is alive and so very real!

Now, if you just look at the raging sea of humanity's corruption, sin, evil, suffering and injustices in the world, then yes, it's true... It's easy to doubt the existence of God with such an overwhelming, darkened visual aspect. But finding faith and coming to know God exists is sort of like one of those 3D stereograms, one of those random dotted pictures where you stare at it for a moment and then an incredible 3D image pops into view.

Yes, if you merely look at the physical universe (the physical dimension) with no consideration that other dimensions or "parallel universes" exist alongside this one, then it is impossible to see or come to know that a real spiritual universe exists all around you. Jesus said, *"God is Spirit and they that worship Him must worship Him in spirit and in truth." John 4:24*

Like the magic 3D image, you have to follow the right protocol or instructions to actually see what appears to be hidden but is actually always right there! Perhaps angle, lighting and the way your eyes adjust their focus helps speed the process of that eureka moment. Likewise, there are human dynamics that must be followed in order for God to clearly come into your visual perspective - where faith becomes sight, where God's presence becomes real and tangible to your own spirit man. You will read the Word of God with new eyes and understand why Christ had to die for all humanity.

The consequence of sin is separation from the Holy God that created you, but Christ stepped in and "did the time for your crime". He paid the penalty for sin with His sacrificial death! Once you see this and cry out in repentance and faith, your whole life will radically change. Hope will rise within you.

You will come to know forgiveness from your sins and freedom from them as well.

Why does God seem to hide himself from us? Because He's not a common thing to just use and abuse for the whims and wants of a wayward mankind. God makes himself rare because He truly is the most precious, most valuable entity in the universe. More precious than gold or silver, He is the hidden treasure that longs for men to seek after and find. Yet in this existential raging sea, God reveals himself to men when conditions are met in the human heart. Jesus said, *"Blessed are the pure in heart, for they shall see God." Matthew 5:8* To really come to know and see God, we must humble ourselves in brokenness and contriteness. Ego and pride are such blind spots to seeing God. God resists the proud but gives grace to the humble. It is when we are no longer resisting His Holy Spirit, no longer justifying our sin and selfishness, no longer enjoying destructive lifestyle choices that are hurting ourselves and others. The sin of pride and rebellion deceives. To experience God's reality we must be willing to give up those things blocking our view of the Almighty.

Yes, the raging sea of darkness, injustice and moral ambiguity will always blind men from ever seeing the clearly evident truth of God's existence and His loving nature.

Do you know the story of Peter with the other disciples when they were in the midst of a raging sea? All they were seeing on that boat was a dark, scary tempest of crashing waves and howling winds. Then Peter saw Jesus, not merely walking on water but transcending a raging, crashing sea below Him! Jesus beckoned Peter to come out of the boat and transcend this raging sea with Him, Peter took the leap of faith and focused His eyes on the Master. As long as he was looking to Jesus, Peter also experienced not merely walking on water, but transcending in that moment the raging sea! Only when Peter began to look away and put his eyes back on the crashing waves did doubt, fear and his own ego crash upon his soul. He began to sink in the raging sea again. But the loving Master would not abandon Peter, even in an hour of doubt and faithlessness. Jesus took Peter's hand and brought him up from the dark and furious waters that wanted to drown him.

If you look at the raging sea around you or even in you, you will begin to doubt, to fear, to lose faith and hope. The world is truly a nasty, lonely, evil, painful and dark place without God in the picture. You will begin to sink in the miry pit of depression, despair, of all that rages around you, the injustices and the suffering. The secular world along with the whisperings of demons and derelicts are always trying to tear down our faith in God and the Master. They constantly want you to focus on the bad, the ugly, the raging sea around you. But the Lord gave us Peter's experience on the raging sea to try to teach us the very secret of truly transcending it!

The secret is simply putting our faith and focus on the Master, on Jesus alone. We can not divert our attention on the raging sea around us or in us.

Remember again, *"These things I have spoken to you, THAT IN ME you might have peace (to transcend the raging sea). In this raging sea (this world) you shall have tribulation: but be of good cheer; I HAVE OVERCOME the raging sea (this world). John 16:33*

Christ clearly teaches us that even as believers we are going to experience tribulation and trials. Even as Christ says, "Peace be still" in our hearts, we are still going to have to deal with the raging sea around us... that is always trying to stir up the raging sea within us. It's a lie to think that coming to Christ means that you will cease from having troubles in your life. Don't listen to any preacher who paints the Christian life in this world as always happy and trouble free. Christians die horrible deaths every day. Their houses burn down. They lose loved ones in tragic accidents. They get flat tires in the pouring rain as they're running late for work. We do not become exempt from trouble, pain, sorrow or injustices. We only see them now as a cross we must bear, as a burden we must share... until the Master destroys the raging sea forever.

Yes, as Christians we transcend much of the raging sea in and around us at times, but none of us are totally free from its grasp until Jesus restores all things. I would be lying to deny that I don't still thrash about, struggling against suffering, stress, temptation and sin alongside all of my brothers and sister like you.

Yet I know that I know that Christ is a real, living and interactive entity on planet Earth. But all my knowing doesn't make you know. I wish faith could be transferred so easily. But the truth is, you must take the leap of faith and also surrender your resistance to God by way of intellectual deceptions. Christ must reveal himself to you.

Now, He doesn't want you to have a "middle man" relationship with Him. He doesn't want you to become religious as in a ritualistic orthodoxy. This circumvents a real and personal relationship with Him and the Father. Many people come to "Christianity" but never to Christ Himself. Many "go to church" but never become the body of Christ, the church, the bride of the Lamb. The difference between true Christianity and the mainstream religion of "Christianity" lies in the living, indwelling presence of Christ. He is so real, living and dynamically interacts with genuine faith, but unfortunately a huge chunk of Christendom merely live in pretense and fakery when it comes down to it. This is mainly due to the corrupted hearts of men who would rather have Christ as an academic concept, an intellectual and historical character than an actual living, Holy Spirit probing entity that they are accountable to on a daily basis.

The devils of Hell would rather make you "twice the child of Hell" by giving you a nicely packaged fake sort of churchianity, where Christ is merely a symbolic figurehead, not the intimate friend and Savior He is meant to be- a churchianity where God may be a grand concept in your intellect and theology but not the personal Father that He longs to be in your life.

If you "believe" with just an intellectual, academic knowledge of God, you're missing out on the reality of His person and the power to transcend the raging sea! The raging sea will eventually destroy the false religious constructs that we build. We will sink because placebo faith (mere intellectual profession) never transcends the raging sea. The personhood of God is a true reality that must be pursued with 100% resolve and really is the only key to overcoming the raging sea.

King David, and all men and women of God in the Bible, learned that God doesn't want our superficial devotion or ritual sacrifices. He wants our hearts. In Psalms 40:6-8 it says, ***"You do not want sacrifices and offerings; you do not ask for animals burned whole on the altar or for sacrifices to take away sins. Instead, you have given me ears to hear you, and so I answered, "Here I am; your instructions for me are in the book of the Law. How I love to do your will, my God! I keep your teachings in my heart."***

You see, He wants to walk with us in an intimate relationship, and in this very truth is the secret to overcoming the world. King David said, *"He brought me up also out of an horrible pit, out of the miry clay, (the raging sea) and set my feet on a rock, and established my goings. And he has put a new song in my mouth, even praise to our God: many shall see it, and fear, and shall trust in the LORD. Blessed is that man that makes the LORD his trust, and respects not the proud, nor such as turn aside to lies." Psalms 40 2-4*

King David walked with God, not perfectly, as we all can stumble and sometimes sink a little in the raging sea, even with true faith. But as we walk with Christ we can change, grow stronger, be transformed. It's a process and a journey. Don't give up even if you fall a thousand times. God knows and is compassionate towards us. He can see the ugly sin and deception that has wrapped its tentacles around our hearts and minds.

Don't let your own flesh, the secular world or demons whisper in your ear that you cannot change or you are hopeless. You can change! People do change every day. We can change through Him! We can become better, stronger, more like the Master. But the secret, again, is focusing on Him. As the scripture declares *"But we all, with open face beholding as in a glass the glory of the Lord, are changed into the same image from glory to glory, even as by the Spirit of the LORD." 2 Corinthians 3:18*

So be patient with God and with your own progress. Character is never developed in a day. God spends great patience in perfecting us, in breaking us and remaking us. He wants mighty oaks, not silly weeds tossed around by every wind or wave.

In the raging sea, character is not born in an instant but rather forged in stages...

Men are either brave or spineless, their hearts cowardly or their hearts courageous.

Just as one can not grow muscle or stamina in a day to fortify his constitution...

So likewise, valiant souls are not made from whim of spirit

170

or impulsive resolution.

True heroes have been heroes long before their moment of bravery and dash...

For God deposits character in souls, from slow endurance not by sudden flash.

David slew Goliath not by slingshot or by five smooth stones that day...

But by a shepherd boy's heart, whom a lion and a bear, he once had to slay.

This is why we suffer, why we struggle, for God our souls to groom...

To truly fly, our wings must strengthen, by breaking out of the cocoon.

The promise is to the overcomers, to those who rise victoriously...

Above the darkness, the storms, the wind, the rain and raging sea.

Comfort and convenience make more cowards than any other affair...

Those with weak constitutions will be the first to fall by snare.

Oh how under heaven, can the righteous be as bold as a lion?

If the least bit of friction or fight, has us crumbling and crying?

Oh precious brethren, the darkness is coming, nay, the darkness is here.

Do we fight from within, from a heart of faith or from a heart of fear?

If you are not a man of principles, of conviction, you will surely give up or betray...

Unless you plead for a miracle from God to change your heart in this last day...

For it has come once again for men to risk it all, for this last time and for all the ages...

I ask you now, will eternity inscribe on you, a heart of a coward or a heart courageous?

None of us can claim to have fully arrived or been completely perfected in this life either. As long as we are in the flesh to experience temptations and trials, we can falter, we can fall. We can sink back down into the raging sea. This is why God warns us to guard our hearts and to be vigilant against allowing evil, self centered thoughts and motives to occupy our minds. ***"Guard or keep your heart with all diligence; for out of it are the issues of life." Proverb 4:23***

The Bible is God's instruction book on how to look to Jesus alone. This is not just a metaphoric phantom gesture. We look to Jesus by looking to His Word and His Spirit, by prayer, by obeying his teachings, learning to deny sinful flesh, our selfishness and our wayward thoughts. ***"Your Word have I hid in my heart, that I might not sin against you." Psalms 119:11***

The battle for our souls actually begins in our minds. Even as we become believers, we need to purge out of our minds old ideas, old philosophies, old lies that the devil has put in us, perhaps years and years of twisted logic and wrong perspectives. We need to discipline our minds by not viewing or fantasizing about things we ought not, casting down vain imaginations. The television, the smart phones, the movie theaters, the computers and video games, they all are trying to captivate our attention and our imagination. Pornography, other smut entertainment and godless media is constantly trying to build a stronghold in our hearts and minds against the knowledge (the knowing) of God.

The only way we can take control of our imaginations and thoughts is by disciplining our minds, (that is, being a disciple) by reading and studying God's Word and only watching wholesome and God honoring media. This is why Paul says, ***"For though we walk in the flesh, we do not war after the flesh: For the weapons of our warfare are not carnal, but mighty through God TO THE PULLING DOWN OF STRONGHOLDS; CASTING DOWN IMAGINATIONS, and every high thing that exalts itself against***

172

the knowledge of God, and bringing into captivity EVERY THOUGHT to the obedience of Christ." 2 Corinthians 10:3-5

Much of the raging sea in us can cease by taking full control of our thought life. Notice Paul didn't say, "Don't worry the Holy Spirit will do all that for you... so just sit back and allow your mind to be flooded with all kinds of filth. God will take care of it." No, Paul gave instructions on how we as believers must take control of our thoughts and cast out of our minds sinful imaginations.

Through obedience to God's Word, not by merely hearing it only, this is how we trust and believe in Jesus. He will ultimately command our hearts, "Peace be still!"

It is so important to guard our hearts and minds from the raging sea of a generation flooded with godless garbage media. Television, Hollywood, Youtube, Facebook, Instagram, Twitter and a host of other social media outlets have turned this generation into a bread and circus age of smut, hedonistic drama and entertainment. We must not allow the raging sea of this tsunami of evil and godlessness into our souls! Networking our hearts and minds into the sewer system of the world will only stir up the raging sea around us and in us. We must come out of Babylon. *"Come out of her, my people, that you be not partakers of her sins, and that ye receive not of her plagues." Revelation 18:4* We will never be able to transcend the raging sea if we allow filth to defile the pure conscience we are to have in Christ Jesus.

I know so many so called Christians who have fallen away from God. Many don't even know it! They think they are okay spiritually! Proverbs 30:12 says, *"There is a generation that are pure in their own eyes, and yet are not washed from their filthiness."*

Because the world and it's philosophies (through Hollywood and mass media) has so deceived them, slowly demoralizing them, the raging sea sometimes rages a slow work of Hell in the soul. Many of them now support the killing of precious unborn babies. They support sexual promiscuity, perversions and lifestyles that are clear abominations in God's Word. This is why we are seeing a great apostasy from traditional, pure Christianity to a "more progressive" inclusive, seeker sensitive "anything goes" Christianity. A Christianity that wants to appease the secularism and lawless hedonism that now rages in our culture.

There's a story about a battleship that was on exercise at sea in very bad weather. It was a raging sea. The captain was on the bridge. It was very foggy. Just after dark, the lookout spotted a light on the starboard side. The captain asked if it was steady or moving. The lookout replied that the light was steady, meaning they were on direct collision course with that ship! The captain ordered the lookout to signal the other ship with these words;

"Change course 20 degrees. We are on collision course."

A signal came back "No. It's advisable for you to change course."

The captain signaled again, "I am a captain. Change course 20 degrees."

"I am a seaman second class. You had better change course 20 degrees," came the reply.

The captain was now furious. He sent back "'I am a battleship! Change course right now!"

A few seconds lingered and then back came this signal, "I am a lighthouse. It's your call mate."

True Christianity and God's holy ways are on a direct collision course with a wicked and perverse generation, bent on corrupting truth and justice. The world, our culture and society are raging against us, saying, "You better change course, Christians! You better become politically correct. You better not preach repentance or try to convict or shame sinners by exposing sin and the unfruitful works of darkness." Change course, we are a battleship that will perhaps destroy your livelihood, ban you from the internet or put you in prison for so called hate crimes (as they condemn our God fearing moral positions as "racism", discrimination and "hate speech"). Or yes, they may even "kill you thinking that they are doing service to God", to rid the world of such antiquated, traditional, fundamental, "bigoted" Christianity. I believe this type of persecution and martyrdom is coming to Christians who won't compromise their faith and convictions.

This Babylonian, end times, worldly system, where "good is now evil and evil is now good", where lawlessness and perversion are called "progressive and liberating", while morality and God's holy ways are despised as controlling and called a form of "racism". Our degenerate culture is an intimidating battleship already, as we are starting to see Christians and pastors put in prison for preaching the gospel or preaching against sin and false religions.

But God's Word is a lighthouse. God's ways can not be compromised or changed, no matter how fast and how far our society spirals out of control towards wickedness and lawlessness. We must stay the course! We must not compromise as many churches and leaders are doing. We must not appease the secular world by conforming to their politically correct demands.

We must not fear man, but fear God alone. If we are to truly win souls and be an effective lighthouse for those lost and drowning in the raging sea, we can not flinch in our resolve and dedication to the Lord, who died for us. Even on threat of death or destitution, we will serve the Lord our God. As Peter and the apostles answered their "battleship" who told them to quit preaching in His name, they replied, ***"We must obey God rather than men." Acts 5:29***

If you think to serve God because you want to be cozy and comfortable in this life, you have a rude awakening coming. This world has always been a place of uncertainty and brokenness. The raging sea will always affect you in this life. There's just no way to circumvent it. But as Christians, it's even more perilous and risky.

As the world grows more evil, the more we crash against this godless culture, the more we will be reviled, threatened, persecuted and condemned. We are seeing this great clash of Christian conservative values play out even now in the present political spectrum. We have to count the cost. Are we willing to know Christ and the fellowship of His suffering? *"Yes, and all that will live godly in Christ Jesus shall suffer persecution." 2 Timothy 3:12* Well, that's not a very cheerful promise from God's Word, is it?

Are we willing to surrender it all to the Master, all our life, our livelihood, our relationships, our possessions? You won't be able to sit on the fence and escape the collision course that's here now and that's coming. You will either compromise, fall and drown in the evil tide rising, or you will stand firm on the rock of Christ, which may cost you everything near and dear in this temporary life. Jesus clearly told us that we would be hated, persecuted and suffer loss in this world for His name's sake.

Besides the unpredictable elements of a raging sea, we also have to deal with a more and more raging anti-Christ worldly system. We are not promised a red carpet treatment in this fallen world.

There's a true story of a strong Christian man who faced unbelievable suffering and loss from the raging sea. Horatio Spafford was a successful lawyer and businessman in Chicago in the late 1800's. He had a lovely family, his wife Anna, and five children. Yet, he was not exempt from the raging sea. His young son died with pneumonia in 1871. In the same year, he lost much of his livelihood and business in the great Chicago fire. Yet he managed to overcome those billowing waves in the raging sea and his business was restored.

Then in 1873, just two years later, the French ocean liner, Ville du Havre, was traveling the Atlantic from the U.S. to Europe. There were 313 passengers on board. Among them were his wife Anna and his four daughters. Horacio had planned to travel with his family, but he ended up staying in Chicago to take care of pressing business matters. He scheduled to meet them in Europe on a later ship.

However, four days into crossing the Atlantic ocean, the Ville du Havre accidentally crashed into the Scottish ship, the

Loch Earn.

Anna brought her four children to the deck as instructed by the ship's staff. She knelt in prayer there with her four daughters, Annie, Margaret Lee, Bessie and Tanetta. They prayed that God would spare their lives. However, minutes later, the Ville du Havre sunk beneath the chilling waters of the Atlantic. 226 passengers including the four Spafford children lost their lives to the raging sea that day.

Anna, Horatio's wife, survived by clinging on to a piece of ship wreckage. She was later retrieved by another vessel. She wired Horatio with this message, "Saved alone, what shall I do?" Another survivor from the tragedy, Pastor Weiss, later told of Anna's grief and yet her faith stood firm. She said, "God gave me four daughters. Now they have been taken from me. Someday I will understand why."

Horatio, in unbelievable anguish and sorrow, went to meet his wife on the next ship available. As they were crossing the ocean, the captain showed Horatio the very spot where the tragedy took place.

Surely Horatio's tears flowed down into the raging sea that took his children. Yet, we know his tears also flowed upwards to the God he knew was faithful and good. Surely he questioned why. Surely he felt the raging sea surrounding him and trying to drown him in sorrow and despair. Yet according to another daughter born after the tragedy, Bertha Spafford Vester, she said that her father, while on that ship alone, as he journeyed to be with his grieving wife, wrote the beloved hymn "It Is Well With My Soul".

Though the raging sea was all around him, Horatio had a tranquil peace that steadied his soul in this world. He wrote these lyrics that have helped countless others brave the raging sea and transcend it's dark and dismal prospect-

"When peace like a river attendeth my way,
When sorrows like sea billows roll,

177

Whatever my lot, Thou hast taught me to say,
It is well, it is well with my soul.
Though Satan should buffet, though trials should come,
Let this blest assurance control,
That Christ hath regarded my helpless estate,
And hath shed His own blood for my soul.
It is well, it is well with my soul."

The truth is, Horatio Spafford learned to trust in God's goodness and faithfulness even when all things looked bleak and despairing. Surely temptation to curse God was there, but Horatio knew the Lord was Lord of the raging sea. He knew that he had not truly lost his daughters, for they were safe and secure in the loving arms of his Master. He would see them again in the eternal habitations of paradise restored.

If our eyes are stayed on the Master, we will make it through the raging sea. We will transcend to walk on the storms and tempests of this life.

Sad as it is to see the scattered ruins of people who succumbed to the raging sea, whose faith now lies shipwrecked in a watery grave, they had been in a fancy delusion that Christianity somehow promised them a happy, trouble free life, when no such promises were ever made. Disillusioned when the raging sea continued to vex them with trial and temptation, they forsook their love and commitment to the Master.

How about you and I? Can we stay the course? Can we keep our eyes on Jesus and resolve to never allow the raging sea to fill us with it's fear, uncertainty and hopelessness?

Say it without any hesitation, any shame or recoil. "I will follow Jesus even if it means I follow Him to be crucified on a cross! If I live, I live for Him alone and if I perish, I perish in Him alone!" This is how we transcend the raging sea. Not by totally circumventing the stormy waters in this ol' world, but by keeping our eyes fixed on Jesus and eternity, our hands firmly grasping His.

Yes, its true- disobedience to truth and God's Word is a fast track to the raging sea swallowing you up. Look at the prophet Jonah. He didn't want to upset the city of Nineveh by preaching against their evil ways. He knew he couldn't compromise and be the cool preacher that speaks fluffy motivational thoughts... or just stay away from the subject of "sin and judgment" since it wasn't trendy. To preach repentance or judgement means you are one of those radical fanatics. You are a "stick in the mud" to their fun and the "party time" spirit everyone is having.

A street preacher of repentance is frowned upon and the other more progressive Christians think they are just uncool, insensitive wannabe prophets. So Jonah disobeyed God and took a ship in the wrong direction. The raging sea prevailed in his life. He put in jeopardy the entire lives of everyone on the ship. Disobedience not only stirs up the raging sea in you but in all those around you. Finally, in desperation, the ship's crew threw Jonah to the stormy waters. God, of course had mercy on Jonah, but first had to teach Jonah that obedience is way easier than the raging sea of disobedience. Sometimes if we feel the raging sea churning up in our lives, we need to do some self examination to see if perhaps disobedience may be the cause.

Yet sometimes the raging sea is also from no fault of our own. It's not due to sin or disobedience. Sometimes God is stirring up a raging sea to direct us in a certain way. Look at Paul the apostle in the book of Acts. He was a prisoner on a ship bound to a certain destination but God had other plans. God stirred up a raging sea and the ship had to crash land at a different destination. God wanted Paul to witness to a group of people who would never have heard the gospel if God hadn't stirred up the raging sea. Sometimes we just have to trust God that the raging sea or trial or tribulation that we are facing will work for His good and testimony... and it will! Sometimes it is painful and hard, but we must keep our eyes on Him.

In closing, I just want to reiterate a vital revelation that if eternity is as long as I can't imagine it will be, then any stress now, even a lifetime of crisis moments or tragedies, after a gazillion years of paradise bliss, it will have diluted our vaporous time on earth in the raging sea to the equivalence of nothingness, of total void. All our struggles, all our pain, no matter how dramatic, emotional or ill-passionate the circumstances in our lives, it is less than one zillionth of a water molecule in a vast eternal ocean of unimaginable peace and paradise. It is therefore wise to be eternally minded. It is in your best interest to be obsessed about eternal things, not finite matters.

Don't allow the temporal raging sea to dictate how you live or react to the circumstances of this life. Do not be of the worldly mindset and "live for the moment". Moments come and moments go; they vanish faster than the blink of an eye.

Live for the forever. If you develop an "eternal awareness" you will live so differently, so concretely, so soberly. The raging sea, that once horrified you with giant sea monsters, will be seen in an eternal light as little nautical creatures that can never put fear or hopelessness in you again. You will react to the stresses and struggles of this life as if they were but a fly on the wall, as if they were such a contemptible, minuscule distraction to your eternal gaze and poise.

You will love more profoundly, more passionately, more abundantly the souls you interface with on a daily basis. You will be anchored in true conviction and discernment against the fleeting trends and the temporal cultures of this world. The passing fads, the whim of a humanity that's lost its way, will seem miserable and unnervingly out of step with the solitude of your eternal consciousness. You will indeed be a solid tree planted by the water's edge. Unshakable. Nothing will move you but what is eternal.

We must draw from within our hearts this eternal perspective. For truly, eternity is already stamped on our hearts, if we but look deep within our souls past the shallow. Pray to God that He gives you the eternal life that comes from knowing Him. Not "eternal life" as in the gift of living forever, this is already a done deal in Christ. But "eternal life" as in living each day with eternity in our hearts. When we do this, the roar of tempest and tide in this mortal zone will infinitely diminish into mere echoes of a raging sea.

HOW TO PLUNGE BACK INTO THE RAGING SEA
(Last Rant For Jesus, I Hope... Maybe...)

In the end, I've shared my heart, this testimony of my life in the raging sea. I've shared how I was rescued by the Rock of Ages, in hopes that others may cling to this same Rock. I know He is more of a reality than the raging sea of this world. I truly hope and pray that you will have a testimony of rescue and redemption also.

In my Christian life, I have tried to plunge myself back into the raging sea for Jesus. I have been part of street preaching ministries where we stood on corners sharing Jesus with lost, drowning men and women. I have been part of ministries where I spoke God's Word to dying drug addicts and homosexuals who had HIV. I have been to third world countries with teams of missionaries where we worked and gave ourselves to reach people with the precious gospel. I have worked with ministries in being caretakers to the mentally ill and handicapped. I have worked in ministries where we provided food, clothing and the Bread of Life for poverty stricken, sin battered souls. We had a thrift store, a food bank and Bible studies for ragamuffin folks. I have written many articles and books published online and offline trying to persuade men with the truth of the gospel.

I share all this not to try to embellish any virtue or "great sacrifices" that I have made. I count my efforts as feeble and lacking, still so contemptible compared to the great love and sacrifice my Lord made for me on the cross.

Since my conversion, it is His Spirit which compels me to try to make a difference in this world. Yet in all my days of trying to rescue, I myself need rescuing as the raging sea, still to this day, batters my soul within and without. I would be a liar and a hypocrite if I tried to paint my life as perfect or struggle free. I still fight to this day with fleshly attitudes and sinful temptations that try to pull me away from God. I still battle with inward character issues like anger, unforgiveness, pride, careless talk and temptations to think evil thoughts. Yes, God has made progress in changing me, and breaking me of many sins, and going after the beggarly elements of this world, but I've not arrived at a state of perfect tranquility and holiness. I am still a work in progress.

If you happen to ever meet me in person and I let you down because you see that I am not a perfect man, or you witness something I might do that is not quite Christlike, please forgive me for still struggling in my raging sea. But also will you do me a favor too- Put your faith in the only One that is perfect and Christlike all the time, Jesus. As for me, you may scold me, rebuke me or encourage me to "practice what I preach". Hopefully I will humble myself and move on from my faults and failures.

I think many prominent Christians, preachers and church leaders do the kingdom of God disservice by always painting themselves as "super spiritual" and almost "sin free", because they want to be perhaps admired and respected as the bling bling of the Kingdom. Not that we should do a bad thing to stay humble or be intentionally sinful to show our humanness, but we should never whitewash our lives with hypocrisy and pretense. We are still just flesh and finite. It's okay to admit this.

If we offend, if we sin, if we get in the flesh, yes, we should be quick to repent. We should be quick to humble ourselves and let everyone know that as long as we are in this raging sea of a world, we will always need the Savior to continually save us. Awesome, right? This way we are relatable to 99% of a fallen, struggling humanity and not paint ourselves as sterling gods to be set on golden pedestals.

The only real reason for any of us to share about our struggles, our sin, our suffering, our pain, is so that we all can throw out a life raft to others in the raging sea... Because they know we are not sitting on some religious high horse judging them, condemning them, but instead we are thrashing about

183

with them, not aimlessly or hopelessly, but thrashing about trying to rescue them with compassion. This is the call of everyone of us, without exception. We are not called out of the raging sea to comfort and convenience. We are all called to plunge ourselves back into the raging sea that we might make a difference in someone's life.

Oh you may not be called to be a Billy Graham. As it was once quipped, *"you may be just one in this world... but you can also be the world to just one"*. Salvation is not about just saving our own skin, but how we can be a brand plucked from the fire to help save others as well.

I want to leave you with the profound vision of William Booth, who was one of the first to define humanity's plight as a raging sea. If you are not on the Rock of Christ, I beg you now to seek Him until you are and then you can be of service to Him in the raging sea. If perhaps you are already rescued and on the Rock, may this deeply move you from being just a spectator to being a participant, plunging yourself back into the sea's hell, to rescue the perishing...

WILLIAM BOOTH'S VISION OF THE RAGING SEA

William Booth wrote (an abridged and paraphrased version), "I saw a dark and raging sea. Over it the black clouds hung heavily; through them every now and then vivid lightning flashed and loud thunder rolled, while the winds moaned, and the waves rose and foamed, towered and broke, only to rise and foam, tower and break again. In that ocean I thought I saw myriads of poor human beings plunging and floating, shouting and shrieking, cursing and struggling and drowning; and as they cursed and screamed, they rose and shrieked again, and then some sank to rise no more.

And I saw out of this dark, angry ocean, a mighty rock that rose up with its summit towering high above the black clouds that overhung the raging sea. And all around the base of this rock I saw a vast platform. Onto this platform, I saw with delight a number of the poor struggling, drowning wretches continually climbing out of the raging sea. And I saw that a few of those, who were already safe on the platform, were helping the poor creatures still in the angry waters to reach the place of safety.

On looking more closely, I found a number of those who had been rescued, industriously working and scheming by ladders, ropes, boats, and other means more effective, to deliver the poor strugglers out of this sea. Here and there were some who actually jumped into the water, regardless of all the consequences, in their passion to "rescue the perishing." And I hardly know which gladdened me most - the sight of the poor drowning people climbing onto the rocks, reaching the place of safety, or the devotion and self-sacrifice of those whose whole beings were wrapped up in the effort for their deliverance.

As I looked on, I saw that the occupants of that platform were quite a mixed company. That is, they were divided into different "sets" or classes, and they occupied themselves with different pleasures and employments. But only a very few of them seemed to make it their business to get the people out of the sea.

But what puzzled me most was the fact that though all of them had been rescued at one time or another from the ocean, nearly everyone seemed to have forgotten all about it. Anyway, it seemed the memory of its darkness and danger no longer troubled them at all. And what seemed equally strange and perplexing to me was that these people did not even seem to have any care - that is, any agonizing care about the poor perishing ones who were struggling and drowning right before their very eyes... many of whom were their own husbands and wives, brothers and sisters, and even their own children.

Now this astonishing unconcern could not have been the result of ignorance or lack of knowledge, because they lived right there in full sight of it all and even talked about it sometimes. Many even went regularly to hear lectures and sermons in which the awful state of these poor drowning creatures was described. I have already said that the occupants of this platform were engaged in different pursuits and pastimes. Some of them were absorbed night and day in trading and business in order to make gain, storing up their savings in boxes, safes, and the like.

Many spent their time in amusing themselves with growing flowers on the side of the rock, others in painting pieces of cloth, or in playing music, or in dressing themselves up in different styles and walking about to be admired. Some occupied themselves chiefly in eating and drinking, others were taken up with arguing about the poor drowning creatures that had already been rescued.

But the thing to me that seemed the most amazing was that those on the platform to whom He called, who heard His voice and felt they ought to obey it - at least they said they did - those who confessed to love Him much and were in full sympathy with Him in the task He had undertaken - who worshipped Him or who professed to do so - were so taken up with their trades and professions, their money saving and pleasures, their families and circles, their religions and arguments about it, and their preparation for going to the mainland, that they did not listen to the cry that came to them from this Wonderful Being who had Himself gone down into the sea. Anyway, if they heard it, they did not heed it. They did not care. And so the multitude went on right before them struggling and shrieking and drowning in the darkness, in the raging sea."

END THOUGHTS
(No really, it is.)

I want to thank you for reading my story, my struggle, My Savior's love for me. I hope I can someday update this book to include many greater wonderful miracles, stories and soul freeing revelations about transcending the raging sea before I shed this mortal clay. Also, thank you so much for your patience with my "Dad rants" too.

I truly pray that you come to know the precious Saviour who is the real secret in transcending the raging sea in your own life.

If you ever feel overwhelmed and need someone to really help you in your struggle, as long as I am available in this world, I resolve to always make myself accessible or to have someone accessible for you. Please feel free to email me on how I can pray with you and for you. The raging sea swallows up too many struggling ragamuffins and I don't ever want to miss an opportunity to help anyone ever again.

Much love, all my precious friends and family. Go with God.   ~ Heath Christopher Goodman
heathcgoodman@gmail.com

About The Author

Heath Christopher Goodman (1967 - ∞) (because he's gonna live forever) was born in Ft Wayne Indiana with birth defects to a few of his fingers, in other words, one of a kind, designer hands. Before that, he survived an attempted abortion. Death has tried to take him out many times since then. However, by God's grace and purposes, he still lingers in this fallen world for only God knows how much longer. He has a passion to give his testimony and promote all of his book's messages. He is a speaker, writer, and business owner. He is a licensed and ordained minister of the gospel, first and foremost by the calling of the Lord Jesus and by the Word of God.

Heath was licensed to preach by his second church, Milton Avenue Baptist Church, Brownwood Texas in 1985 at the age of 18 and ordained by the Missionary Methodist Church while attending Youth With A Mission in the late 1990s. He has labored with several ministries through the years such as Youth With A Mission, Last Days Ministries (Kieth Green's ministry), His Touch Ministries, A.L.A.R.M. (A Longing After Revival Ministry), Breckenridge Village, Calvary Commission, Christian Community Fellowship, The Cross Worship Ministry and My Brother's Keeper Charities & Missions. Heath truly loves doing missionary work and evangelism. He is available to give his testimony, speak passionately on the abortion issue or to preach the whole counsel of God in a spirit of love and mercy. He resides in a suburb of Atlanta Georgia with his wife, Marivania, his daughter Jordanna and son Joshua.

He can be contacted directly by email at;
heathcgoodman@gmail.com

LEAVE YOUR MARK ON THE WORLD.
GET YOUR BOOK PUBLISHED TODAY!

Do you have a book inside you? Of course you do!

Everyone of us has a testimony or a story. Everyone of us has a lesson learned that could be turned into a story or teaching moment.

We need Christian authors who want to inspire and touch the lives of others through their Christian writing. There is such a void in this world for God-fearing, morality based stories for our children and for adults. We need you to help raise up the standard of truth and purity before the Lord!

Whether it is fiction or nonfiction, a children's book or for all of us big kids, we want to help you edit, illustrate and publish or "self publish" your God inspired, "heart-of-fire" literary masterpiece! Contact us now!

Get your book formatted, cover illustrated and printed within as little as a few weeks for a great price! You can utilize our pre-release Christian publishing service for anyone who wishes to get their draft book or manuscript printed as a book with a full color cover illustration. The pre release edition of your book can be used as a way to generate interest, serve as a "feedback release copy", give as gifts and even to submit it to other larger publishers as a concept release manuscript.

Or we can help you fully publish your book under our own publishing company, Creative Works Press. We do it all- from book formatting to cover design to acquiring ISBN numbers to printing copies to putting your book online in any format to reach millions of people and bookstores!

We do not retain any rights or royalties over your work. We can do a turn key service of designing, editing, formatting, printing and shipping a set number of copies to you. You market and sell your books however you wish. ISBN services and a website for your book are also available.

Creative Works Press is dedicated to being a high quality Christian publisher and bringing material that promote God honoring, beautiful, uplifting messages to it's readers. Like any publisher, we reserve the right to publish only material that identifies with our Christian mission statement and core values. Contact us today for a free consultation!

Creative Works Press
2001 Duncan Dr. NW Ste. #44
Kennesaw, GA 30156
404-307-9185
sales@creatorgraphics.com
www.CreativeWorks.cloud

CREATIVE
WORKS
PRESS

Leave Your Mark On The World.

From A Raging Sea To A Raging Sea

God sets our feet upon a rock from a raging, stormy sea...
Far from the struggles or crashing waves, so glad we are set free...
We pray, read the Word, worship and even fast as our heart's devotion...
Yet God shatters our pious rituals and asks, "Is this what I have Chosen?
Is it not to feed the hungry, give shelter and clothing to the poor?
But you say, "Be warmed and filled" and yet do nothing more.
Is it not to set the captives free and heal hearts so hurt and broken?
Instead you do religious things and pray prayers so very token.
Yes, God called us out of the raging sea to heal us and make us whole...
But only to call us to plunge back in, to rescue the drowning souls...
Sure it seems like we must battle again the wind, the waves and rain.
Yet all our sacrifices will pale in the light of what we will forever gain.
No, the raging sea is not a threat to undo our steadfast love for Christ...
Instead, it is the greatest opportunity to manifest this abundant life.

~ Heath Christopher Goodman

*"Isn't this the fast that I have chosen: to break the chains of wickedness,
to untie the cords of the yoke, to set the oppressed free and tear off
every yoke?
Isn't it to share your bread with the hungry, to bring the poor and
homeless into your home, to clothe the naked when you see him,
and not to turn away from your own flesh and blood?
Then your light will break forth like the dawn, and your healing will
come quickly. Your righteousness will go before you, and the glory of
the LORD will be your rear guard." Isaiah 58: 6-8*